AF506125

Liberalism and the Defence of Political Constructivism

Liberalism and the Defence of Political Constructivism

Catriona McKinnon
Lecturer in Political Philosophy
University of York, UK

First published 2002 by
PALGRAVE MACMILLAN
Houndmills, Basingstoke, Hampshire RG21 6XS and
175 Fifth Avenue, New York, N.Y. 10010
Companies and representatives throughout the world

PALGRAVE MACMILLAN is the global academic imprint of the Palgrave Macmillan division of St. Martin's Press, LLC and of Palgrave Macmillan Ltd. Macmillan® is a registered trademark in the United States, United Kingdom and other countries. Palgrave is a registered trademark in the European Union and other countries.

ISBN 0–333–96507–8

This book is printed on paper suitable for recycling and made from fully managed and sustained forest sources.

A catalogue record for this book is available from the British Library.

Library of Congress Cataloging-in-Publication Data

McKinnon, Catriona.
      Liberalism and the defence of political constructivism /
      Catriona McKinnon.
           p. cm.
      Includes bibliographical references and index.
      ISBN 0–333–96507–8 (cloth)
        1. Liberalism. 2. Constructivism (Philosophy) 3. Justification
      (Theory of knowledge) I. Title.

      JC574 .M43 2002
      320′.01′1–dc21   2002073541

10   9   8   7   6   5   4   3   2   1
11   10   09   08   07   06   05   04   03   02

Printed and bound in Great Britain by
Antony Rowe Ltd, Chippenham and Eastbourne

Contents

Preface and Acknowledgements

This book addresses a worry about liberalism which has been amplified in recent years in various well-worn criticisms of liberal political justification; in particular, of Rawlsian political justification. The source of these criticisms is that such justification only successfully addresses people who are already committed to liberal political principles or liberal values; that is, liberal political justification gives reasons for action only to people who are already committed liberals. This criticism has reared its head in various strands of contemporary political thought. It can be seen as an aspect of the (now waning) communitarian approach to political justification. Here, the justification of political principles must start with the values embedded in the practices and traditions of communities to whom political justification is addressed, on the grounds that these values are constitutive of the identity of community members, and political justification must take seriously the identity of those it addresses. Communitarians often attacked liberalism by claiming that liberals assume that people to whom their political justifications are addressed are capable of standing back from the values embedded in their communities in order to critically assess them, and that this assumption reveals a defunct and metaphysically suspect conception of the person as an 'unencumbered' self.[1] The spirit of the communitarian attack on the liberal conception of the person is echoed across various approaches which purport to challenge the liberal paradigm of political justification. We find it in some forms of 'multiculturalism' which advocate the communitarian 'constitutive' conception of identity, but accord special significance to identities constituted by membership of cultural communities.[2] It is also present in some feminist critiques of liberalism which turn on the claim that the moral reasoning attributed to the persons to whom liberal justification is addressed reflects an 'ethic of justice' associated with male moral development; thus, liberal political justification has a built-in bias against women and their moral concerns.[3] Finally, the criticism seems to have bolstered some 'post-modernist' rejections of the possibility of non-relativist political justification. For example,

Richard Rorty accepts the communitarian criticism but is unapologetic on the grounds that political justification can do nothing other than address those with whom we share values and beliefs, in which case liberal justification can do nothing but address liberals.[4]

I think that most of these criticisms of contemporary liberal political justification rest on sloppy or wilful misreadings of the canonical texts of contemporary liberalism. Since the publication of John Rawls' *A Theory of Justice* in 1971,[5] many liberals inspired by this book have been explicitly and self-consciously trying to construct political justifications that do not rely on assumptions that the people to whom these justifications are addressed share the same secular, humanist, Enlightenment values. To present such liberal thinkers as ignorant of or insensitive to the demand that the context of political justification is pluralistic is crass and boring: I shall not be addressing any of the versions of the well-worn criticism laid out in the last paragraph in this book.

However, the well-worn criticism can be seen as an overstated response to a more subtle concern about the nature of contemporary liberal political justification. To see this concern we need to accept two things, and accept that most contemporary liberals accept these things. (1) All political justification must start with some assumptions about those to whom it is addressed, even if these are just that the addressees do not reject the possibility of justification, and are in circumstances which make the need for principles of justice pressing. (2) The circumstances in which the political justification of principles of justice is a pressing need are permanently pluralistic: the people to whom political justification is addressed are ineliminably diverse in their beliefs, values, and desires. Given (1) and (2), the question for liberals is: what assumptions about the persons to whom political justification is addressed make the justification of liberal principles possible, consistent with an acceptance of the permanent fact of pluralism? The danger for liberals who accept (1) and (2) is that the assumptions about persons required for liberal principles to be justified to these persons undermine a commitment to the permanence of pluralism. The worry is that justifying liberal principles requires a set of assumptions about persons which severely narrows the range of diversity in any society in which liberal principles are justified, and that this legitimises creeping doubts about whether contemporary liberal political justification has any role to play in a world populated by people more diverse than such justification can acknowledge.

In this book I map out and criticise what is taken by many political philosophers to be the best attempt to address this concern: John Rawls' political Constructivism. While I endorse the structure and aims of Rawls' Constructivist justification, I think that some of the assumptions about persons which inform it raise the concern laid out in the last paragraph. However, I think that the best aspects of Rawls' Constructivism can be retained, and this concern addressed, once we substitute for Rawls' problematical assumptions a set of assumptions about persons as committed to their self-respect and its social conditions. By making this substitution, Rawlsian Constructivist justification can yield liberal principles without raising the subtle concern of the last paragraph; and an added bonus of this is that the hysterical expressions of this concern can also be put to rest. My aim in this book, then, is to present an interpretation of Rawls' political Constructivism which avoids the accusation that Rawlsian liberalism simply preaches to the converted. This interpretation will rest on giving a more prominent role to an idea already present in Rawls' thought: that self-respect and its social bases are values fit to appear in the political justification of liberal principles in a pluralistic world.

I have been working on this book in one form or another since 1994, and I have been extraordinarily lucky in having the support of many kind and generous friends – colleagues or otherwise – along the way. The book started life at University College London as my Ph.D thesis. Although what appears on these pages has moved a long way from that, I would never have had the motivation or interest to carry on with this without the excellent supervision of Véronique Muñoz-Dardé and Jo Wolff during that time. I am deeply grateful to both of them (hopefully they will see some progress here!).

After taking a job in the Department of Politics at the University of Exeter I finished my thesis and started to turn it into a book. All of my colleagues in the Politics department were understanding about my attempts to do this while getting to grips with a new job, and I would like to thank them for it. However, I am particularly grateful to Dario Castiglione and Iain Hampsher-Monk. Dario and Iain created time for me to get on with this by taking tasks upon themselves, notwithstanding their own already onerous commitments, and were without fail supportive, encouraging and good for a laugh. I would also like to thank Nigel Pleasants at Exeter for his sympathetic ear when I wound up complaining about the book. Having just turned his own Ph.D thesis into a book, his advice was gold dust. I would not have been able to get a contract for this book without the help of these people, and I would like to thank them warmly.

In my current post in the Department of Politics at the University of York I have again struck oil. Of my colleagues here I would particularly like to thank Matt Matravers and Sue Mendus. Sue externally examined my Ph.D thesis in 1998; Tom Pink was my internal examiner, and I would like to thank him for this. At the time, Sue gave me extremely helpful, acute and constructive comments on my work, and she has continued to do so ever since. She has been a constant source of guidance and encouragement to me over the last few years in ways that go far beyond the call of duty. I would like to thank her warmly for her support and friendship. I would also like to thank Matt Matravers for his comments on this book, and for his help and advice since my arrival in York. Matt's comments on my manuscript were hard hitting, detailed and often very funny. I know I have not addressed all of them here, but I am nevertheless enormously grateful to him for making them: they came at a time when I had run out of steam, and I would not have made the final push without them.

The staff at Palgrave Macmillan are also due thanks. In particular, I would like to thank Alison Howson for her cheerful toleration of my pushing back of deadlines, and for her strictness in giving me a final deadline when it mattered. She has been a source of good advice throughout the whole process. I would also like to thank Hillel Steiner, and an anonymous reader, for their helpful and constructive comments on an early version of the manuscript.

Finally, I would like to thank my family and friends. There were some hard times for me while I was writing this book, and I would not have got through them unscathed without the love, affection, loyalty and clear vision of a number of people for whom I care deeply. My family have been an unswerving life-line: I would like to thank my dad, Jim McKinnon, my sister, Fiona McKinnon, her partner, Pete Wardell, and I would also like to welcome the latest addition to the clan McKinnon, Madeleine McKinnon-Wardell. I would like to thank the friends already mentioned above in professional contexts and, in addition, the following people, for all the things that really matter: Karen Chung, Ian Cross, Cécile Laborde, Bice Maiguashca, and Neil Storer. In particular, I would like to thank Jeremy Moss for Beijing and everything since.

I would like to thank the AHRB for a Research Leave grant which supported my work on this book, and the University of York for an additional term of research leave.

CATRIONA MCKINNON

1
Introduction: The Practice of Political Justification

1.1 Introduction

Political justifications are everywhere. They are most obvious in the places where people are employed to construct, challenge and analyse them: parliament, think-tanks, the news media and academia. But they are also a fundamental part of every person's life, including people who proclaim their boredom with politics, and their lack of interest in how they are governed. It is not only people like civil disobedients, trade union and party activists, politicians and pundits who are involved in the exchange of reasons that constitutes political justification. Also involved is everyone who has ever voiced an opinion on whether Britain should adopt the Euro, the US Star Wars programme, the war in Afghanistan, the state of the National Health Service and the price of petrol. When people talk about political issues they do not simply state their preferences, as they would when talking about holiday destinations or menu choices. Rather, they attempt to convince and persuade one another, and most of the time they use reasons rather than violence: 'Britain should reject the Euro because it will bring closer integration into Europe, which will threaten sovereignty and national identity'; 'The Star Wars programme should be avoided because it will fuel another arms race'; 'income tax should be increased to fund improvements in the NHS'; 'the war in Afghanistan is illegal and immoral'; 'government taxes on petrol for hauliers should be kept as they are because of the damage their vehicles cause to the environment'. These kinds of statements are not technical tools available only to specially trained political analysts and advocates. Rather, they are the sorts of considerations that people offer to one another in support of their opinions, in a world in which they cannot avoid forming some opinions on some political issues. When people do this they are engaged in political justification; questions of political justification are questions for everyone.

This said, my aim in this book is not to address political justifications as they appear in everyday life. Although I think that people cannot avoid engaging in political justification completely, it is also true that they are more than political animals, and have the rest of their lives to attend to. This means that everyday political justifications are often not subtle or interesting from a philosophical point of view, although they doubtless have more of an effect in the world of *realpolitik* than philosophical political justifications. Nevertheless, my interest here is in a form of philosophical political justification. Although I believe that there is no difference in kind between the practice of everyday political justification and the practice of philosophical justification, philosophical political justifications ultimately raise deep questions about the nature of justificatory value in political society that are not – or, at least, not explicitly – raised by everyday political justifications. I shall address some of these questions in this book.

Let me start by way of introduction in this chapter by specifying how I shall understand the term 'political justification'. Here, I shall take political justification to be a matter of using arguments to persuade those addressed by the justification to accept certain political principles freely (call this the 'practical' conception of political justification). The arguments involved in practical political justification need not exhibit the sophistry of the politician, the technique of the philosopher, or the learning of the lawyer. Instead, what the term 'argument' signifies is the offer of reasons for accepting or rejecting certain proposals to those to whom the justification is addressed. A person mounting a political justification aims to persuade those she addresses that they have good reasons to accept her political proposals. A political justification offered by a person who aims to persuade those she addresses is successful when it is fit to convince those it addresses that they have these reasons. Philosophical problems of political justification relate to what constitutes a good argument in this context. This chapter will introduce some of these problems and map how they are addressed by the dominant philosophical theories of practical political justification. Let me first say a little more about the practical conception of political justification in general.

Political justification involves the exchange of reasons. But what sorts of reasons? The reasons exchanged in the arguments constitutive of political justification aim to change, or be fit to change, the way people behave. A person mounting a political justification aims to convince those she addresses to modify their behaviour in accordance with her proposals, and to convince those addressed that it is legitimate to use force against those who do not restrain themselves in this way: her means of persuasion are reasons which will, or are fit to, change the behaviour of those she addresses without the use of force. It is the action-guiding aspect of political justification that raises various interesting philosophical questions. However, let me first make some brief remarks on the theoretical aspects of political justification.

If political justification must be acceptable to people in its theoretical aspects, and if it is ultimately action-guiding, then it must be framed in terms that people are able to understand: call this the 'intelligibility' constraint. Strangely, this constraint is hardly ever made explicit by political thinkers, perhaps because they think it too obvious to state.[1] Everyday political justifications tend to meet the intelligibility constraint. If philosophical political justifications should ultimately inform everyday political justifications (otherwise, what would be their point?), then philosophical political justifications must also be subject to the constraint. However, the intelligibility constraint applies less stringently to philosophical political justifications. This is because these justifications are usually interpreted by politicians, pundits and commentators before they are presented to the public in everyday political justifications, and we can (hopefully) expect higher levels of tolerance for technicality, and a greater degree of expertise, among such interpreters.

The intelligibility constraint requires a conception of the likely limits of the theoretical understanding of people addressed by political justification, or an account of how well-informed on certain subjects we can reasonably expect people to be. These expectations set the limits of what it is possible for people to understand. Political justifications requiring Einstein's understanding of physics will be ruled out on any account. But by going too far in the other direction the constraint runs the risk of 'dumbing down' political justifications.

For example, if it is thought unreasonable to expect that people are capable of grasping the concept of Pareto-efficiency then certain political justifications of some principles of economic redistribution will be hard to make.[2] Or, if it is thought unreasonable to expect people to understand the basic processes by which global warming occurs then some justifications of global environmental approaches will be ruled out. The limits of what it is possible for people to accept from a practical perspective will in part be set by a conception of the limits of human theoretical understanding, combined with an account of what it is reasonable to expect people in the audience for a political justification to learn, given that they are not only members of an audience for this justification, but also parents, friends, lovers, siblings and colleagues, where all of these roles make demands on their time and can clash with their commitment to acquire the knowledge necessary for them to engage in justificatory debate.

Remaining within the theoretical perspective, not only must justificatory arguments be intelligible, they must also be sound, and supported by evidence where appropriate. With respect to soundness, I shall assume that the basic principles of logic apply. The question of what constitutes sufficient evidence for a particular claim appearing in a justificatory argument will vary according to whether the claim is scientific, historical, sociological, economic, psychological, etc. These are questions that cannot be addressed in this book.

Turning to the action-guiding aspect of political justification, justificatory reasons must normally take precedence over other reasons in practical reasoning. Political justification aims to convince people that either they ought to restrain themselves according to its principles, or that the coercion used to restrain those who do not restrain themselves is legitimate. This means that the reasons it offers must – or must be fit to – defeat any other competing reasons that people have. Without this requirement a justificatory reason would be just one more reason in a person's set of competing reasons for action. But justificatory reasons are supposed to have a special feature: they are supposed to guide the action of disparate people in order to co-ordinate their behaviour according to a set of rules or principles. Unless justificatory reasons normally – or are normally fit to – defeat other practical reasons, they will not serve this purpose.[3] So, not only must justificatory reasons be 'motivationally adequate' (that is, be fit to motivate people to act for them), they must also normally defeat any other motivationally adequate reasons a person has. That justificatory reasons defeat other reasons with which they may conflict does not mean that they should be thought of as *cancelling out* these other reasons: justificatory reasons do not fill the space of all reasons. In that case, a set of justificatory reasons can be successful for a group of people divided with respect to all their other practical reasons; members of the group can accept and give precedence to justificatory reasons without a convergence of reasons elsewhere in their sets of reasons.

The question of how justificatory reasons could take priority over other reasons without cancelling them out is a question for anyone who thinks that political justification should yield reasons which are reasons for all people. The problem of how this is possible becomes especially acute once justificatory reasons are characterised as impartial, and therefore can require that a person not act on her partial reasons. For example, when a justificatory reason requires that a person not pull strings at her local Housing Authority to ensure that her daughter jumps to the top of the queue for public housing, or that a person does not pervert the course of justice to protect her husband from a criminal prosecution. The questions of why justificatory reasons should take priority over other reasons, and how they can do so, are among the stickiest in contemporary political philosophy, and I shall not be addressing them here. Rather, I just stipulate that justificatory reasons must take such priority. If it turns out that they cannot then political justification as I conceive it is not possible.[4] My main interest here will be in the motivational adequacy of justificatory reasons, where this is not understood as a question about how these reasons can take priority over partial reasons.

Different conceptions of political justification operate with different criteria of motivational adequacy for justificatory reasons. And different sets of problems arise depending on which set of criteria for motivational adequacy is endorsed (see section 1.3). The motivational adequacy constraint expresses the practical aspect of political justification, and the intelligibility constraint expresses its theoretical aspect.

A final general point about political justification relates to what it is that is justified by such arguments. There are two broad subjects which are addressed by political justification. First, political justification might address the existence, nature and extent of state power and, if successful, establish political obligations: questions addressed by these justifications are questions of political legitimacy. Second, a justification might address political principles or procedures: these are questions of justice. Different criteria of justificatory success can be applied to questions of legitimacy and of justice within the same overall theory of justice, and the success of a political justification addressing questions of legitimacy does not imply the success of another political justification within the same theory addressing questions of justice.[5] To put it bluntly, a legitimate state need not be one which enacts just legislation. My focus in this book will be on how questions of justice are justified: I shall have nothing to say about questions of legitimacy.

Now that I have made it clear what will not be discussed in this book, let me outline what will be discussed. I start from the assumption that political justifications are practical and unavoidable. Granting this, the following sets of questions can be used to distinguish different conceptions of political justification (section 1.1). Who is addressed by the political justification? Call this the question of 'scope' (section 1.2). Must justificatory reasons actually be accepted for a political justification to succeed? Or is it enough for the success of a justification that people could accept – or would accept – its reasons? What does it take for a justificatory reason to be fit to motivate those it addresses? Call these questions of 'justificatory success' and 'motivational adequacy' (section 1.3). What sorts of values must be expressed by justificatory reasons? How do these values affect the scope and success of justifications, and the motivational adequacy of their reasons? Approaches to the question of value in political justification can be classified as Pragmatist, Perfectionist and Constructivist. Although different traditions of political justification can be distinguished according to their answers to these questions, it is also the case that different strands within traditions can answer these questions differently. The tradition of political justification I shall address in this book is liberalism, and I shall distinguish between different strands of this tradition by focusing on these three questions (section 1.4).

1.2 Scope and diversity

Let me call the set of people to whom a political justification is addressed, and whose responses to it determine its success or failure, the 'constituency' for that political justification. At the limit, the boundaries of a political justification might map on to the boundaries of the world, in which case it has a cosmopolitan constituency. In this case, political justification transcends state and community boundaries; here, the distinction between domestic and global perspectives with respect to the issue of justice in question is rejected (and is sometimes claimed to be nothing but a convenient artifice which can be used as an excuse for ignoring uncomfortable questions of what we owe to distant strangers as a matter of justice).[6] No one advocates a cosmopolitan constituency for all political justifications; some justifications legitimately address non-global constituencies of justification, which may or may not map on to state or community boundaries. What makes those who call themselves 'cosmopolitans' distinctive is their general suspicion of the relevance of state- or community-based restrictions on constituencies of justification, and their consequent demands that such restrictions be argued for rather than just assumed.

A further question of scope relates not to the global or local scope of a constituency, but rather to who gets included in it, regardless of whether it is global or local. Cosmopolitan and local constituencies of justification can be divided according to whether all adult, mentally competent members of the cosmopolitan or local group are included in the constituency. What I shall call 'inclusive' constituencies of justification incorporate all members of the group making up the constituency, and exclude only children and the mentally incompetent. In contrast, 'exclusive' constituencies exclude various categories of people beyond children and the mentally incompetent who are genuine members of this group.

Highly exclusive constituencies of political justification have been the norm for most of human history. Exclusive constituencies are often elitist: those whose responses to the political justification determine its success are a group who view themselves as worthy of, and those they exclude as unworthy of, political justification. In the past, members of such groups have been identified by the colour of their skin, their ethnicity, their lineage, their property rights, their class, their sex or their religion. Exclusive constituencies of justification often make for unstable societies. Where swathes of those affected by political proposals are not invited into justificatory debate – because justificatory arguments are not addressed to them – civil unrest and possibly revolution are the likely outcome, even if the principles justified to the exclusive constituency are in fact good principles. Of course, justifications addressing exclusive constituencies very often relate to bad principles: they address a constituency of limited scope precisely because of their interest in exploiting and oppressing those outside of the constituency.

However, exclusive constituencies do not necessarily aim at the oppression of those they exclude. An exclusive constituency can sometimes indicate a sense among those in the constituency that they have been oppressed and exploited by those with whom they refuse to enter into justificatory dialogue. An exclusive constituency is sometimes justified by those in it as a form of protection against those who will not participate in justificatory dialogue in good faith, those who aim to weaken the solidarity between members of the constituency. Class-based Marxist constituencies can exhibit this feature ('*Workers* of the world unite!'), as can radical feminist constituencies which include only women (and sometimes only lesbian women), and religion-based groups such as The Nation of Islam.

What sorts of constituencies do liberal political justifications address? With respect to the question of whether constituencies should have cosmopolitan or local scope, liberals are divided.[7] The debate among liberals about the virtues and vices of cosmopolitanism is continuing, and not settled: I shall not be addressing it here. However, with respect to questions about who gets included in the constituency, whatever its size, liberals are united. All liberal forms of political justification operate with inclusive constituencies of justification: this is one of their most distinctive features. As Jeremy Waldron puts it, 'Liberals demand that the social order should in principle be capable of explaining itself at the tribunal of each person's understanding.'[8] No person who possesses understanding should be excluded from the constituency of justification, and liberals have argued that qualities like skin colour, sex, religion and lineage, for example, have no bearing on a person's capacity to use her reason in the assessment of political justifications.

A second distinctive aspect of contemporary constituencies of justification for many liberals is that they are taken to be deeply diverse, and permanently so. Contemporary liberal theorists of political justification accept a constraint on political justification that liberals like Locke, Rousseau, Kant and J. S. Mill did not recognise, or at least, not explicitly. This constraint is that the deep differences on questions of value and morality between those to whom political justification is addressed cannot be expected to disappear under ideal conditions: deep diversity is ineradicable. The term 'deep diversity' indicates more than disagreement about the content of morality and beliefs about value; it also indicates disagreement with respect to the source of value and the authority of morality. Most liberals accept that disagreement on these questions is probably permanent; many liberals think that this fact is not to be regretted; and some liberals find it a cause for celebration.

The contemporary liberal understanding of deep diversity differs from historical liberal understandings in its insistence on the fact that deep difference is *ineradicable* in conditions of freedom and justice. However, liberals differ in their explanations of why deep diversity is ineradicable in such conditions, and they also differ in their attitudes to ineradicable deep diversity. The most common explanations of, and attitudes towards, diversity found among contemporary liberals are as follows.

(1) *Deep diversity is the normal result of the exercise of reason in conditions of freedom, and is not be regretted.* This is the view of John Rawls and Brian Barry. Rawls thinks that some form of deep diversity is ineradicable in virtue of certain 'burdens' that the exercise of judgement stands under. The complex nature of empirical evidence bearing on hard questions, disagreements about the importance of various pieces of evidence, the vagueness of concepts, the effect of biography on the interpretation of evidence and argument, the complex nature of competing normative considerations, and the limited 'social space' in which competing views can find expression all mean that the exercise of reason in conditions of freedom cannot be expected to lead to agreement on moral, religious and philosophical questions.[9] (I shall discuss and criticise Rawls' conception of the burdens of judgement in more detail in Chapter 2, section 2.4.)

Brian Barry's explanation of deep diversity as the normal result of the exercise of reason under freedom relies on the 'denial of the legitimacy of certainty' with respect to the views which constitute diversity.[10] This mild form of scepticism makes the imposition of any view upon others by political means illegitimate. Such scepticism is demanded, thinks Barry, by reflecting on the history of disagreement. All the means of persuasion employed by one party to a disagreement to convince the other party to change its mind – whether these be war and torture, or teaching and conversation – have spectacularly failed to produce convergence. But, he asks, '[i]f I concede that I have no way of convincing others, should that not also lead to a dent in my own certainty?'[11] Admitting that it should lead to such a dent makes a person's refusal to use political means to impose her views on others reasonable. Given this restraint, which supports the protection of conditions of freedom, we can expect that reasonable people will continue to fail to convince one another of their views.

The key difference between Rawls' and Barry's conceptions of diversity as ineliminable, even given the normal and proper exercise of reason, is the degree of diversity construed as reasonable on each view, with Rawls making allowance for a far greater degree of reasonable diversity than Barry. Their differences here are particularly acute with respect to religion. Rawls claims that his account does not, 'question the possible truth of affirmations of faith [and above] all it does not argue that we should be hesitant and uncertain, much less skeptical, about our own beliefs'.[12] Barry, on the other hand, characterises religious beliefs as 'dogmatic slumbers',[13] and argues instead that anyone with the sceptical attitude engendered by the proper use of reason should be happy for their ideas to, 'take [their] chances in competition with other ideas': the suggestion here is that religious beliefs would not fare well in such a competition.[14]

(2) *Deep diversity is the normal outcome of the exercise of reason given that values are incommensurable, and is not to be regretted.* This is the view of Isaiah Berlin and, partly, of Joseph Raz.[15] To say that two values are incommensurable is either to say (a) that the ways of life associated with each are not practically compatible, such that the pursuit of one rules out the pursuit of another, and they cannot be pursued at the same time; or to say (b) that the values cannot be compared and ranked in terms of their value, whether by reference to another value or not; or to say (c) that both (a) and (b) are true of the values in question. If these theses of incommensurability are true then the pursuit of one way of life rules out a myriad of others, and many of the choices we make between valuable things cannot be guided by considerations about which of these things is the most valuable: we must choose on other grounds. If we are given freedom to make our choices there is no value which presents itself to us as a guide to the others, and many paths we take permanently rule out other paths.[16]

This means that deep diversity is ineradicable. We are all faced with choices between incommensurable options, and given that there are no master-values, we cannot all be expected to choose in the same way. As this is just a fact about what it is to be a being capable of valuing and choosing, there is nothing to be regretted about the fact and permanence of deep diversity.

(3) *Deep diversity is the normal outcome of the search for identity in conditions of freedom, and is to be celebrated.* This is the view of Will Kymlicka, and some other liberal multiculturalists.[17] According to Kymlicka, the diverse cultural groupings which contribute to deep diversity provide a context essential for the maintenance and development of a particular identity. Given that people cannot be expected to converge on one set of particular pursuits peculiar to one cultural context, any liberal approach sensitive to the importance of identity will provide principles fit to protect cultural contexts as necessary for the protection of identity. Multiculturalist accounts of deep diversity are only partial: they explain the value of deep diversity, but another explanation is needed to show why people cannot be expected to converge on the pursuits and practices which inform their identity, perhaps as in (1) or (2). What multiculturalist approaches add is a reason to value deep diversity not given by (1) or (2).

(4) *Deep diversity reflects the total contingency of values and history in the modern world, and is to be celebrated.* This is the view of Richard Rorty, and assorted 'post-modernists'. On his account, deep diversity is a feature of a world that has woken up to the illusions of Greek, Christian, and Enlightenment foundationalism. The myths of universal truth, God, an ahistorical human nature and the unifying power of Reason have, thinks Rorty, rightly been abandoned. What is left is a collection of human animals utterly separated by their self-understandings and different languages of interpretation. Rorty thinks that liberal solidarity ought to be cultivated in groups of these animals, but not at the cost of the reintroduction of chimerical foundations; the most we can do is attempt to persuade others of liberal values with beguiling stories, and hope that they are beguiled. As deep diversity signals humankind's escape from myths and philosophical fantasies, it is to be celebrated.[18]

(5) *Deep diversity is the face of a fractured post-modernity in which the lodestone of shared traditions has been lost, and is to be regretted.* This is a view on the edge of liberalism. It is most often associated with Alasdair MacIntyre, who calls for a return to an Aristotelian tradition

of ethics and politics (to be precise, a Thomist tradition), rather than the acceptance or embrace of deep diversity so characteristic of liberalism.[19] Notwithstanding his rejection of what he takes to be liberal values – autonomy, unfettered choice, self-reinvention, market freedom – MacIntyre does not advocate a *forced* return to a Thomist tradition; he does not advocate the use of state coercion to inculcate Thomist values. MacIntyre shares with liberals a rejection of the use of state power to promote religious, moral and philosophical ends, even if he would prefer a world in which all people shared Thomist ends and values. Although ineradicable, deep diversity reflects the flaws in many people's value systems, and their failure to come to know the moral truth, and thus is to be regretted.

Some liberals think that the permanence of deep diversity is due to epistemic (or some other kind of) failure on the part of people who fail to hold the correct values or acknowledge their real source or authority, and consequently have a view of political justification as a form of instruction, as a way of educating people into these values. In this book I shall argue for a form of political justification which avoids such judgements. Liberal political philosophers who make such judgements think that without an account of moral truth, political justifications lack firm ground on which to stand, and from which to resist anti-liberal political justifications. For example, unless liberal political justification allows us to say to a person who denies equal voting rights to women that some of her beliefs are false and her values flawed, liberal political justification is too weak to protect liberal political institutions.[20]

This view of liberal political justification does not involve a denial of the permanence of deep diversity; but it does involve judgements about whether it is to be regretted. If deep diversity incorporates anti-liberal views which are premised on false beliefs and flawed value systems, then deep diversity is to be regretted. In this book I aim to defend a form of practical political justification – a form of Constructivism, to be specific – which minimises the need for such judgements. This form of political justification allows us to argue that liberal principles are justified without making judgements about the falsity of anti-liberal beliefs, or the flaws in anti-liberal value-systems. At least, it aims to minimise the number of such judgements, and limits their subject matter. Constructivism, as I shall develop it, aims to provide each person with reasons for accepting liberal principles while minimising the number of judgements required of the values, beliefs, and practices of the people to whom political justification is addressed. The liberal Constructivism I shall develop stands opposed to the idea of political justification as a form of instruction.

Why is this an attractive aim? As I have already mentioned, I believe that philosophical political justifications must be framed with an eye to becoming everyday political justifications. Without such framing, philosophical political justifications are idle and speculative; interesting to philosophers, perhaps, but of no real significance with respect to the state of the world which they purport to aim to change. If we accept that philosophical political justifications should be translatable into everyday justifications which explicitly aim to change the world, then the question of the audience for such justifications arises. This audience is permanently and deeply diverse. The question then is: are political justifications which rest on a disputed account of the moral truth, or morality's authority, fit to motivate people to act for the reasons they present? For such reasons to become motivating for all persons would require that all persons accept the truth of the same moral theory underlying the justification, and accord to this theory the same authority.

Political philosophers who take truth-oriented approaches to political justification are likely just to nod their heads at this point: truth is truth, and in an ideal world all people would see truth as truth. Although venerable, this way of thinking about political justification has created a stalemate in the project of political justification, with those who (let us assume) know the truth on one side, and the recalcitrant and deeply diverse world of flawed reasoners on the other. Something has gone seriously wrong here. Unless we deny that political justification should be action-guiding, or unless we insist that truth-based political justifications are action-guiding because it is not logically impossible that all persons will come to see the moral truth, and act for reasons informed by it, we should look for another approach. This approach will be sensitive to what it would take for a set of reasons to become motivating, in the light of a real commitment to the permanence of pluralism: it will avoid presenting justificatory reasons to a deeply diverse world as a *fait accompli*, in a take-it-or-leave-it manner. Rather, this approach searches for reasons which could become motivating for all while minimising the diminishment of deep diversity in its ideal constituency of justification. I shall return to these issues in section 1.3, where I distinguish between different accounts of what it takes for a reason to be motivationally adequate, and show how the 'demandingness' of justificatory reasons becomes an issue for those – like advocates of the truth-based approach to political justification – who think that people should always adjust to justificatory reasons, rather than reasons sometimes adjusting to persons.

Liberals operate with inclusive constituencies of justification which they accept as permanently diverse in the ways I have outlined. However, it is also the case that liberals aim for a degree of critical distance with respect to the practices and traditions of actual communities in the world. This means that liberal justifications aim to do more than simply articulate the values of existing constituencies of justification; at least, if such articulation is all they aim for, liberals accept that it needs to be argued that this is all that they can aim for. The critical distance for which liberals aim is revealed in another shared commitment: liberal justificatory reasons must be informed by, and must express, the value of equal individual liberty. Although this commitment encompasses disagreement about the range of liberties which might be taken to inform liberal reasons, and the principles which might be adopted in addition to principles of equal liberty,[21] it is nevertheless a commitment which enables liberals to be united in their opposition to justifications wherein political goods like stability, average utility, national prosperity or the identity of a particular community within political society demand the infringement of individual rights or restrictions on liberties.[22]

To sum up, in this book I aim to give an account of how we can construct critical, action-guiding political justifications which can be addressed to people in inclusive constituencies of justification which are deeply and ineradicably diverse. There are three main ways in which the values and reasons of such justifications might be conceived. Before outlining these approaches I want to say a little more about the different ways in which justificatory reasons can be conceived of as successful and action-guiding.

1.3   Justificatory success and motivational adequacy

What does it take for a political justification to be successful? Are successful justificatory reasons ones that people would accept, could accept, or could not reject, under a specified set of conditions? There are at least three criteria of justificatory success corresponding to different answers to these questions.

The 'hypothetical-acceptance' criterion:
A political justification succeeds if and only if its justificatory reasons *would be accepted* by members of the constituency of justification, were they to be presented with them.

The 'possible-acceptance' criterion:
A political justification succeeds if and only if its justificatory reasons *could be* accepted by members of the constituency of justification.

The 'impossible-rejection' criterion:
A political justification succeeds if and only if its justificatory reasons *could not be rejected* by members of the constituency of justification.

The hypothetical-acceptance and impossible-rejection criteria contain the possible-acceptance criterion, if the latter is understood (trivially) as stating that there must be a possible world in which justificatory reasons are accepted. Justificatory reasons can only be hypothetically accepted if it is possible for them to be accepted; and a set of reasons that could not be rejected must be one that could be accepted. In that case, the possible-acceptance criterion of justificatory success is common to all conceptions of political justification. So, what marks the difference between conceptions of justificatory success is the question of whether hypothetical-acceptance or impossible-rejection is the appropriate criterion of justificatory success.

It might be objected that there is no real distinction to be made between a reason which would be accepted by a person P in conditions C, and a reason which could not be rejected by P in C. The thought here is that whatever could not be rejected by P would be accepted by P. One way to respond is to paint hypothetical-acceptance in more active terms than non-rejection; we might claim that the fact that P would accept R means that P would willingly embrace R (or something along these lines), whereas the fact that P could not reject R is consistent with P accepting R begrudgingly, with bad grace. I am not sure whether such a distinction is sustainable. In any case, in what follows I shall be treating impossible-rejection as the criterion of justificatory success: to show that a set of reasons could not be rejected by a constituency of people gives sufficient justification for implementing the proposals that the reasons support. If hypothetical-acceptance is distinct from non-rejection, then the fact that members of this constituency would only accept these reasons begrudgingly or with bad grace is neither here nor there from a moral point of view.

The problem with the impossible-rejection criterion of justificatory success is that it does not specify the grounds on which the impossibility of a set of reasons being rejected confers success on the justification in which the reasons appear. It might be the case that, holding a gun to the head of Fred, Fred could not reject the reasons I give him for doing what I want, but we would hardly say that my proposal has been justified to Fred in these conditions. Persons can be made incapable of rejecting reasons through all sorts of measures which we would think are inappropriate in political justification: brain-washing, hypnotism, coercion, threats, etc. So in order to employ an impossible-rejection criterion of justificatory success a theory of political justification must provide an account of the grounds of non-rejection which explains why a person's standing in that relation to a justificatory reason makes the justification in which it appears a success. The assumptions about persons – their psychology (moral and otherwise), what they value, how they value and how they reason – map the boundaries of the psychological, reasonable and ethical possibilities within which political justifications operate. Much of the work of the philosophy of political justification is taken up by spelling out and defending these assumptions, as we shall see when we come to examine Perfectionist, Pragmatist and Constructivist accounts of justificatory value and the motivational adequacy of justificatory reasons.

A further feature of successful justificatory reasons given a practical conception of political justification is that they must be fit to motivate people to act for these reasons; they must be action-guiding. Justificatory reasons must be motivationally adequate because political justification is a practical activity: it ultimately aims to convince people that either they ought to restrain themselves according to its principles, or that the coercion used to restrain those who do not restrain themselves is legitimate. A reason which was not fit to motivate people to act could not be a practical reason.

Let me pause here to flag three ways of conceiving of motivational adequacy. One way – sub-Humean internalism – avoids problems of demandingness but raises questions about the critical power of political justification. The others – externalism and (what I shall call) 'deliberative internalism' – answer worries about critical distance, but raise questions about demandingness. Let me explain how.

First, it might be claimed that justificatory reasons are only fit to motivate people when they connect in an interesting way with the motivational commitments people presently have: this is 'internalism' about practical reasons. Or second, it might be claimed that justificatory reasons can be motivationally adequate even when they do not connect with persons' present motivational commitments: this is 'externalism' about practical reasons. Let me be more precise about internalism and externalism; in particular, about the two broad varieties of internalism which, with externalism, constitute the three approaches to motivational adequacy I shall consider.[23]

Internalism about practical reasons

A practical reason to Φ is motivationally adequate for a person P if and only if

(a) P has a present motivational commitment to Φ, or
(b) P would have such a commitment were she to deliberate soundly from her present motivational commitments, where
(c) a sound deliberative route to the commitment to Φ may or may not be constrained by P's present motivational commitments.[24]

The 'sub-Humean' version of internalism is expressed in clause (a): a reason is motivationally adequate if and only if acting on it would promote the satisfaction of at least one of an agent's present desires or fulfil at least one of her present motivational commitments. Because this view counter intuitively entails that we can never say of a person that she has reason to do something unless she desires or is already explicitly committed to doing it, many people reject sub-Humean internalism. The alternative is to construe the motivational adequacy of any practical reason to Φ in terms of whether P would acquire a motivation to Φ were she to deliberate soundly from her present motivational commitments; that is, what I shall call 'deliberative' internalists assert clauses (b) and (c) in the outline above in addition to (a).

Externalism about practical reasons

A practical reason to Φ can be motivationally adequate for a person P even if

(a) P does not have a present motivational commitment to Φ, or
(b) P would not acquire such a commitment if she were to deliberate soundly from her present motivational commitments, where
(c) a sound deliberative route to the commitment to Φ may or may not be constrained by P's present motivational commitments.[25]

The difference between internalism *per se* and externalism is just that externalists allow for the possibility that some reasons can be fit to motivate a person without connecting in an interesting way with their present motivational commitments. Disagreements between internalists and externalists are mostly over the nature of the deliberation required for motivational adequacy,[26] and the nature and content of the motivational commitments in terms of which internalists characterise motivational adequacy.[27] The philosophical literature on the internalism/externalism debate *per se* is large and technical and I do not propose to survey it here. In any case, I shall not be treating the fact that a theory of political justification is committed to internalism or externalism *per se* as grounds for criticism of that theory. Instead, the relevance of the three-fold distinction between sub-Humean internalism, deliberative internalism and externalism to the assessment of competing theories of political justification is laid out below.

I conceive of political justification as unavoidable, practical, and – for liberals – addressed to a constituency which is inclusive but nevertheless accepted as permanently deeply diverse; political justification should present critically potent justificatory reasons to such a constituency. If a theory of political justification takes a sub-Humean approach to the motivational adequacy of justificatory reasons then it faces the following question.

(S-Hi) Do members of the liberal constituency presently have the motivational commitments necessary for justificatory reasons to become motivating for them?

If members do presently have these commitments the next question is:

(S-Hii) What is it about these present commitments which makes them appropriate as constraints on justificatory reasons?

The danger for liberals who employ sub-Humean internalist criteria is that the present motivational commitments which place motivational adequacy constraints on prospective justificatory reasons can rob those reasons of their critical potency. If constituency members' present commitments are nefarious, and these constrain what counts as a justificatory reason, then justification cannot gain the distance necessary for criticism of these nefarious commitments.

To avoid this conclusion, and to secure the possibility of critical potency for practical reasons, many internalists advocate a form of deliberative internalism over sub-Humean internalism. Here, the claim is that reasons are motivationally adequate when people would acquire a motivational commitment to act for these reasons, were they to deliberate soundly from their present motivational commitments. The other alternative to the sub-Humean view is an externalist account, as follows.

If members do not presently have the commitments referred to in (S-Hi) then the theory must be employing externalist criteria of motivational adequacy. A theory of justification is externalist about the motivational adequacy of justificatory reasons when it allows that these reasons can be fit to motivate people regardless of their present motivational commitments. To see the problem that externalists face, we have to be clear about what externalists deny, that is: no reason can be motivationally adequate without connecting in an interesting way with a person's present motivational commitments. This denial does not imply (a) that motivationally adequate reasons *cannot* be adequate by connecting with a person's present commitments, or (b) that a person who acts for a reason R *must* do so in the absence of a motivational commitment to act for R. What the most plausible externalists claim is that it is possible for deliberation about a reason to *create* a motivational commitment to act for this reason where this deliberation does not proceed from, and is not constrained by, a person's present motivational commitments. Thus, externalists about justificatory reasons claim that a justification can be acceptable to persons even if they lack present motivational commitments to act for the justificatory reasons it contains, so long as reflection on these reasons creates motivational commitments to act on them. Notwithstanding this distinction between internalism and externalism, both externalism and deliberative internalism face the same set of questions about motivational adequacy.

(E/DI-i) Is it possible for persons in the liberal constituency of justification to acquire the motivational commitments necessary for action according to justificatory reasons without contradiction or inconsistency?

If this is possible the next question is:

(E/DI-ii) How demanding are the motivational commitments which must be acquired by members of the liberal constituency in order for them to be motivated to act for justificatory reasons?

The first question relates to what I shall call the 'formal' aspect of motivational adequacy, and the second question relates to the 'demandingness' aspect of motivational adequacy. The danger for liberals who employ externalist or deliberative internalist criteria of motivational adequacy is that even when it is possible for persons to accept justificatory reasons without contradiction or inconsistency, the motivational commitments persons must acquire to act for these reasons are too demanding, given that the liberal constituency is permanently and deeply diverse, and given that we want political justifications which have a chance of making the changes they aim at through translation into everyday political justifications. That is, the serious question for liberals employing these criteria is expressed in (E/DI-ii). For contemporary liberals addressing deeply and permanently diverse inclusive constituencies of justification, reasons which demand the acquisition of radically new motivational commitments – or commitments which can only be acquired as a result of difficult, subtle and extended deliberation from present commitments – in order to be motivationally adequate cast the liberal claim to accept the permanence of deep diversity in a suspicious light. Highly demanding reasons would seem to narrow the range of diversity taken to be ineradicable in the constituency: the worry then arises that liberal justifications merely preach to the converted, that is, those who are already presently committed to acting for liberal justificatory reasons. If so, then it looks like sub-Humean criteria of motivational adequacy are being employed, as it were, by default.

To review, formal questions of motivational adequacy *per se* relate to whether a justificatory reason *could be* motivating for a person, and here there is a split between externalists on the one side, and sub-Humean and deliberative internalists on the other. But questions of demandingness relate to what it would take for a reason for which people *could* act to become a reason for which they *do* act: the split here is between sub-Humean internalists on the one side, and externalists and deliberative internalists on the other. Given a sub-Humean internalist account of motivational adequacy, justificatory reasons are not demanding because persons must already have a motivational commitment to act for the reasons for them to be considered adequate in the first place. Deliberative internalist accounts make justificatory reasons more demanding than this because reasons must be accepted in virtue of sound deliberation from a person's present motivational commitments, and sound deliberation is not something that all persons are presently committed to. The question of demandingness also arises for externalist accounts of motivational adequacy, where the worry about demandingness is that the changes that would have to be wrought in members of the constituency in order for them to acquire the appropriate motivational commitments are radical, deep and wholesale. In that case, notwithstanding the formal motivational adequacy of a justification employing externalist criteria of motivational adequacy, the sense in which the practical reasons it offers are action-guiding is unclear. The mere formal possibility that reasons could be accepted seems to lack practical justificatory potential when the motivational commitments necessary for action on these reasons are very demanding.

More needs to be said about the idea of demandingness in this context. When I say that a theory of justificatory value is too demanding I shall mean that it requires an objectionably high degree of uniformity along some dimension by reference to which justificatory reasons might become motivating. My claim will not be that justificatory reasons should be undemanding, because one test of the critical power of justificatory reasons is whether they make demands of members of the constituency of justification. That is, many critically potent reasons will make demands of members of the constituency, and rightfully so. Rather, the important question is what level of demandingness is objectionable. This is – and can only be – a delicate matter of judgement: I shall make no attempt to set out necessary and sufficient conditions for objectionable demandingness. Rather, I shall (in Chapter 2) compare the levels of demandingness of different sets of justificatory reasons, and recommend a set that is the least demanding. Let me isolate the dimensions according to which a theory of justificatory value can be demanding, by way of illustration.

These dimensions are routes to motivational adequacy for deliberative internalists and externalists; that is, they are the areas in which people might change so as to acquire motivational commitments to act for any justificatory reason (either through sound deliberation from their present commitments, or via the creation of new commitments bearing no relation to the person's present commitments). There are at least four basic dimensions of uniformity that a demanding theory of justificatory value can require: belief, desire, motivation and character. Let me say something about each of these dimensions.

1. Belief

A theory of justificatory value is demanding along the dimension of belief when, in order for justificatory reasons expressing these values to become motivating, a person must acquire beliefs about what is good and/or true. Beliefs can play this role when motivation is conceived of as a matter of the interaction between certain beliefs and desires. For example, that I desire a glass of wine, and that I believe there is a bottle in the fridge, explains why I am motivated to get up and go to the fridge. A theory of justificatory value becomes more demanding as the number of beliefs people must share in order to be motivated to act for justificatory reasons informed by these values increases. For example, a theory of justificatory value according to which justificatory reasons become motivating only when all members of the constituency of justification share a set of religious beliefs is very demanding.

2. Desire

As with belief, a theory of justificatory value which is demanding in terms of desire operates with a belief–desire theory of motivation. And again, as with belief, the demandingness of such a theory increases as the number of desires it requires to be shared in order for justificatory reasons to become motivating increases. For example, a theory of justificatory value is very demanding along the dimension of desire when it requires that all persons want a secular state in order for justificatory reasons to become motivating.

3. Motivation

The third category in which justificatory reasons can make demands is that of motivation, where this is not understood in terms of the interaction between beliefs and desires. This category is necessary because there might be theories of motivation other than the belief–desire theory. For example, some externalist thinkers argue that reasons can become motivating through a process not related to reflection on, or deliberation from, present motivational commitments, and that the motivation which is created by this process need not be conceived of as a desire. A theory of justificatory value is very demanding along this dimension if, for example, it requires that what motivates all people to act for justificatory reasons is a commitment to progress and the pursuit of higher pleasures, where this commitment is either not analysed in terms of the interaction between beliefs and desires, or is given an alternative analysis.

4. Character

The final way in which justificatory reasons can be demanding is by requiring that all persons share aspects of character in order that the reasons become motivating for each of them. Character is a matter of settled dispositions, preferences and tastes, standards of behaviour, ideals and patterns of judgement. Character is an amalgam of a person's features which distinguish her from others with whom she may share beliefs, desires and motivations. A theory of justificatory value is demanding along this dimension when it requires all persons to have a similar character in order for justificatory reasons to become motivating for them. For example, justificatory reasons which require that all people have a sense of themselves as primarily public and political beings is very demanding.

In summary, political justifications which take the fact of permanent deep diversity as their starting point, and aim at inclusiveness, face this question: is there a critically potent – and yet not overly demanding – theory of justificatory value fit for political justification to such a constituency? I shall argue that a form of Constructivism which takes self-respect as its fundamental value fits this bill; or, at least, fits it better than the other dominant Constructivist theories of justificatory value in the literature. For the remainder of this chapter, let me make some introductory remarks about how Constructivism contrasts with the other two dominant approaches to justificatory value, Perfectionism and Pragmatism.

1.4 Perfectionism, Pragmatism and Constructivism

There are three broad categories of value that can inform the reasons of political justification: Pragmatist, Perfectionist and Constructivist. Let me consider these approaches in this order.

Pragmatists think that the constituency for any justification maps on to an actual community in the world with a history, and shared practices. Pragmatist values are found in actual, shared traditions and practices in the world as it is, and Pragmatist political justifications are framed in terms of reasons which express shared values. Pragmatists reject political justifications which articulate values which are not in a significant sense shared by all members of the constituency for the justification which, according to them, can only map on to some real, existing community. Because of their focus on local tradition and existing practice, Pragmatism is sometimes claimed to be the approach to political justification which takes deep diversity most seriously: there are as many Pragmatist constituencies of justification as there are actual communities facing different political problems in the world as it is.

Pragmatists take motivational adequacy to be internalist: to be successful, justificatory reasons must connect in an interesting way with the present motivational commitments of members of constituencies found in actual communities. In framing justificatory reasons to be presented to these constituencies, Pragmatists claim to dispense with ideal assumptions about the grounds on which persons accept reasons. Pragmatists claim instead that justificatory reasons should track the present motivational commitments of persons in various constituencies realised in actual communities with shared histories and traditions. In this way, they claim, no one is excluded from the constituency of justification. This strategy is particularly evident in the work of Richard Rorty.

There are at least two grounds on which to criticise the Pragmatist strategy for avoiding problems associated with internalist criteria of motivational adequacy. First, when political justification tracks present motivational commitments it loses the critical distance characteristic of liberal justifications, and to that extent it is unclear that Pragmatist strategies of justification are suitable for liberals who need such critical distance to justify a principle of equal liberty. And second, the assumption that members of actual, discrete communities constituting liberal constituencies do, in fact, share certain motivational commitments is in any case implausible. In that case, some assumptions must be made about the grounds on which justificatory reasons are acceptable to persons, and the expectation must be that people in constituencies who fail according to these ideals ought to acquire the motivation to act for these reasons, either by reflection on their present motivational commitments, or by reflection on the reasons themselves, so as to be in a position to act for justificatory reasons. But this means that justificatory reasons are now taken to be motivationally adequate according to externalist, or deliberative internalist, criteria in which case questions of demandingness arise.

The historically dominant externalist account of justificatory values and reasons is Perfectionism. For Perfectionists, justificatory values count as values only from the perspective of a particular moral theory, or religious faith, and they are expressed in reasons upon which people ought to act as a matter of morality or salvation. Because Perfectionist political justifications are driven by strong, 'top–down' conceptions of what people ought to do, they can have an air of exclusionary paternalism to them which looks immediately inconsistent with liberal inclusiveness: it is best for people to live according to *these* principles, regardless of whether they accept the truth of this or not. However, it would be a mistake to assimilate Perfectionism to paternalism, because more sophisticated Perfectionist accounts of justificatory value are possible. For example, a liberal Perfectionist might be committed to the justificatory value of social co-operation according to Christian values, but refuse to exclude non-Christians from the constituency of justification on the grounds that the only effective way to convert these people is by including them in justificatory debate informed by Christian values. One such Perfectionist is Joseph Raz, who takes the value of personal autonomy to justify liberal principles.[28]

If we assume that Perfectionist reasons are motivationally adequate with respect to the formal aspect of externalist criteria, the worry about Perfectionism relates to the demandingness of Perfectionist justificatory reasons. If, in order for justificatory reasons to become reasons for which members of a constituency of justification act, all members have to acquire the same religious beliefs or accept the truth of the same moral theory, then the diversity taken to be a permanent feature of liberal constituencies is significantly diminished. It is not that the limits that Perfectionism places on diversity are objectionable just in themselves: all forms of political justification fit to yield critically potent reasons place some limits on diversity. Rather, what is worrying is that these limits are set in the name of religious or moral truth. When political justification becomes a form of instruction – however benign the intentions of the instructors – liberals should start to worry. Some of the greatest political atrocities in history have been performed in the name of instructing dissenters into moral truth. A form of political justification which yields liberal results without delivering the firebrand of moral truth into the hands of those who already wield political power is to be preferred, if such an alternative exists.

The preferable alternative to Perfectionism is Constructivism. The question with which Constructivists start is: what can we legitimately assume that people facing unavoidable and practical problems of justice must value? Constructivism differs from Perfectionism because its justificatory values are vindicated without reference to a true moral theory or faith, but rather through consideration of what has to be assumed about persons if they are to act at all: the values of Constructivist political justification are ideas of practical reason. Constructivism differs from Pragmatism because the claim is not that justificatory values are vindicated in virtue of being shared by actual persons. Constructivists thus reject sub-Humean internalism. Does this mean that Constructivism operates with externalist criteria of motivational adequacy? Much depends on the conception of the person at the heart of Constructivist justification, from which justificatory values are constructed. Some Constructivists are deliberative internalists: they claim that justificatory values are those that people would be committed to were they to deliberate soundly from their present commitments. Other Constructivists are externalists: they allow that justificatory values need bear no relation to persons' present motivational commitments. Either way, Constructivists face questions of demandingness with respect to their account of justificatory reasons.

Constructivist accounts of justificatory value can be empiricist, non-empiricist or political. Empiricist accounts construe justificatory values in terms of a set of desires which, it is argued, people share in virtue of their shared agency, personhood or practical reason.[29] For example, Charles Taylor argues that human agency is characterised by the activity of 'strong evaluation', whereby human beings have second-order desires, expressed in a deep and articulate language, that certain of

their first-order desires be satisfied.[30] The capacity for strong evaluation (along with certain other important capacities) can only be
developed in certain social contexts (this is Taylor's 'social thesis').[31]
Therefore, in virtue of having the second-order desires constitutive of
strong evaluation, all people must value the social contexts in which
the capacity for these desires can be exercised, and these contexts
deserve political protection.

Non-empiricist accounts construe justificatory values in terms of
a set of reasons people share in virtue of features they share other
than desires, and are on the whole Kantian accounts.[32] For example,
Onora O'Neill argues that a political commitment to the avoidance
of systematic and gratuitous injury can be constructed from features
abstracted from the practical reason shared by all persons. O'Neill's
Constructivism avoids empiricism because she does not characterise
successful practical reasoning in terms of the satisfaction of desires, or
of getting what one wants. Instead, practical reason is characterised
by her in terms of certain assumptions which must underlie the
behaviour of any agent who can be genuinely said to act at all.[33]

Finally, political Constructivists – like John Rawls – attempt to
isolate shared features of persons *qua* citizens in both empiricist
and non-empiricist terms. Rawls' Constructivist starting point is the
question of what persons exercising their practical reason to solve
the unavoidable problems of justice they face together must value
(it is the restriction Rawls imposes that justificatory values are to
be derived only from a consideration of practical reason *as it addresses
questions of justice* that makes his Constructivism political). With these
values isolated, justificatory reasons can be constructed from them.
The question for Rawls upon which I shall focus is whether these reasons are too demanding. I shall argue that Rawls' Constructivism can
be made less demanding and still justify liberal principles once we
drop the requirement that persons facing problems of justice together
must accept that their judgement operates under burdens, and replace
it with the requirement that such persons care about their self-respect
and its social conditions, and accept that all other people do so too.

The book as a whole proceeds as follows. In Chapter 2 I outline
Rawls' Constructivism and show the way in which Rawlsian Constructivist reasons are demanding. At the end of Chapter 2 sketch
my version of a less demanding liberal Constructivism. The sketch
is fleshed out in Chapters 3 and 4. In Chapter 3 I give an account of

self-respect and its social conditions. In Chapter 4 I argue that a conception of persons as caring about their self-respect and its social conditions is an idea of practical reason as it addresses questions of justice, and furthermore that reasons for endorsing characteristically liberal procedures of justification could not be rejected by persons conceived of as self-respecting. Chapter 5 suggests how self-respect based Constructivist justification might affect the justification of political principles of equal liberty and economic justice, and some problems which arise given this perspective of justification.

2
Constructivism in Rawls

2.1 Introduction

In *A Theory of Justice* Rawls offers a detailed argument for three fundamental principles of justice – distributing equal basic liberties, equal opportunities and maximin income and wealth[1] – derived from the following general conception of 'justice as fairness'.

> All social primary goods – liberty and opportunity, income and wealth, and the bases of self-respect – are to be distributed equally unless an unequal distribution of any or all of these goods is to the advantage of the least favoured.[2]

Apart from some modifications to the first principle of equal liberty,[3] and changes to the way in which primary goods are conceived of as appropriate goods for distribution by principles of justice,[4] Rawls retains his commitment to justice as fairness in *Political Liberalism*. What *Political Liberalism* is largely concerned with, and the points on which it differs from *A Theory of Justice*, relate to the question of how to conceive of the well-ordered society and the persons who populate it for the purposes of political justification. A conception of the person, and her society as well-ordered is, for Rawls, a presupposition of the justification of any political principles: we start by imagining the ideal case in which such principles could be justified, and give an account of these principles (and subsequently a constitution, and political institutions) in this ideal case, before proceeding to work out how these principles apply to non-ideal and real cases.[5]

We start by working within what Rawls calls 'ideal theory', where we assume that the society for which we seek principles is well-ordered. The conception of the person and society which constitute Rawls' conception of the well-ordered society in *Political Liberalism* are a set of assumptions which underlie his political justification and, in combination with a certain procedure of construction, constitute his theory of justificatory value. In this chapter I shall lay out this theory, and argue that it is more demanding than it needs to be: if an alternative, less demanding theory of justificatory value could be found that would deliver the same results then that theory is preferable to Rawls'. I sketch such a theory towards the end of this chapter, and flesh it out in Chapters 3 and 4.

2.2   Ideal theory: structure and issues

Rawls states that,

> [T]he principles of political justice may be represented as the outcome of a certain procedure of construction. In this procedure … rational agents, as representatives of citizens and subject to reasonable conditions, select the public principles of justice to regulate the basic structure of society. This procedure … embodies all the relevant requirements of practical reason and shows how the principles of justice follow from the principles of practical reason in union with conceptions of society and person, themselves ideas of practical reason.[6]

The details of the conception of the person from which justificatory reasons are constructed are justified, Rawls thinks, on the grounds that unless persons are thought of as having these features they could not be thought of as exercising their practical reason to address the problems of justice they unavoidably face together. In *A Theory of Justice* this procedure of construction was given by the device of the original position; here, representatives of citizens are placed behind a 'veil of ignorance' which ensures that their choice of principles is rational and reasonable.[7] The device of the original position is not repudiated in *Political Liberalism*, but it is not prominent. Rawls thinks that the procedure of construction in this book, and the conceptions of the person and society which inform it, 'provide political liberalism with an appropriate conception of objectivity'.[8] Rawls' Constructivism aims to provide objective political justifications which do not rely, as in Perfectionism, on a true moral theory according to which justificatory reasons are appropriate, nor, as in Pragmatism, on tying justificatory reasons to the values and practices of actual communities. So, what is Rawls' Constructivist procedure of justification? And what are the conceptions of the person and society that inform it?

Rawls claims that:

> Justice as fairness is best presented in two stages. In the first stage it is worked out as a freestanding political (but of course moral) conception for the basic structure of society. Only with this done and its content – its principles of justice and ideals – provisionally on hand do we take up, in the second stage, the problem of whether justice as fairness is sufficiently stable. Unless it is so, it is not a satisfactory political conception of justice and it must be in some way revised.[9]

At stage 1, the aim is to 'set out justice as fairness as a freestanding view, an account of a political conception of justice that applies in the first instance to the basic structure and articulates two kinds of political values, those of political justice and of public reason'.[10] Stage 1 involves the articulation of principles of justice without reference to any particular moral, religious or philosophical views. Instead, stage 1 principles are constructed on the basis of the commitments of stage 2 persons, who are thought of as practical reasoners facing unavoidable problems of justice together, but who differ on questions of morality, value, religion and philosophy.

It must be stressed that stage 2 is part of the apparatus of normative political justification: stage 2 is not a description of what people are actually like, or of how they are likely to develop. Noting this helps to avoid misplaced criticisms of Rawls. The ideal persons to whom justificatory reasons are offered at stage 2 are in conditions of *reasonable* pluralism, and clearly these are not the conditions of the world as it is. Nevertheless, some commentators have treated stage 2 as descriptive in the sense of being predictive, and have claimed that Rawls' political justification fails because the predictions it makes at stage 2 are false: people are not likely to transform themselves into the ideal people to whom Rawls' justification is addressed at stage 2, so this political justification is unlikely ever to be accepted by real people.

Leif Wenar advocates just such a reading of Rawls. According to Wenar, stage 2 should be treated as a test of whether the conception of justice articulated at stage 1 will be *likely* to gain acceptance among people with comprehensive commitments in the liberal constituency of justification. On this view, the reassurance we ask for at stage 2 is motivated by 'the difficulties of winning general agreement, and the transition costs of reforming institutions [which make us] under-standably reluctant to bother with proposed political changes that will unravel as soon as instituted'.[11] On the 'likelihood' reading of stage 2, justification is successful only when we are able to predict that people in the world as it is are likely to accept the justifica-tory reasons presented to them; in other words, Rawls' Constructivist justification succeeds only if it is likely that members of the con-stituency of justification will realise the ideal of the person laid out at stage 2. This interpretation is evident in Wenar's claim that, 'Very few comprehensive views, as we now know them or can expect them to become, *will* support justice as fairness as Rawls describes it', on the grounds that, 'Rawls' presentation of justice as fairness is based on a conception of the reasonable that a variety of comprehensive doctrines, as we know them and can expect them to become, *will* reject'.[12]

Given this reading, Wenar argues that practitioners of the major world religions, like Roman Catholicism, are unlikely ever to accept Rawls' political justifications because of the requirement (which Wenar imputes to Rawls) that arguments of faith do not enter political justifi-cation. Wenar claims that this requirement is tantamount to a demand that 'fundamental aspects of [Roman Catholics'] faith and their atti-tude toward it' be abandoned.[13] What are these aspects and attitudes? Wenar claims that Rawls' political justification requires acceptance of 'the difficulty of finding the truth even under the best conditions',[14] or 'the difficulties of making correct judgments about values and facts'; accepting this, Catholics and other religious people must accept that their religious beliefs are nothing but articles of faith, and that others cannot be expected to accept political justifications reliant on these beliefs.[15] But, Wenar argues, given that it is a fundamental part of Catholic doctrine that 'those religious truths which are by their nature accessible to human reason can be known by all men with ease, with solid certitude, and with no trace of error, even in the present state of the human race',[16] the expectation that those engaged in political justification do not conceive of their beliefs as the only true beliefs on that subject excludes devout Roman Catholics from the constituency of justification. Wenar claims that many world religions demand the same degree of certitude from devotees as is demanded by Roman Catholicism, which undermines the likelihood that Rawls' conception of justice will be accepted by such religious believers.

Wenar's attack on Rawls, and others like it, can be met once stage 2 is read as part of the normative apparatus of political justification, and not as a comment on what people are like, or how we can expect them to develop. As Thomas Hill reflects, the acceptance of justificatory reasons at stage 2 requires that persons understand the grounds according to which the conception of justice is articulated at stage 1, understand that all other potential participants also understand these grounds, and accept that this conception ought to shape their basic political institutions. It also demands that the reasons citizens have for this acceptance prevent the collapse of stability in the face of changes to the balance of power in the society (this prevents overlapping consensus from being a mere *modus vivendi*). If stage 2 is a prediction then, based on the evidence we have about how people behave now, it is a bad one. Hill claims that the complexity of issues involved in stage 1 articulation, the persistence of disagreement on political matters, and the ubiquity of non-rational grounds for stability in those societies that are stable, make it highly unlikely that the overlapping consensus described in *Political Liberalism* will ever become a reality.

So, what we need is a reading of stage 2 whereby it does not test the probability of stage 1 justificatory reasons being accepted. Instead, stage 2 must be interpreted as a test of the normative force of stage 1 reasons, where this is understood as constituted in part by their motivational adequacy. If stage 1 reasons could not be rejected by stage 2 ideal people, then we can measure the demands action for such reasons imposes on actual people by comparing the depth of diversity in the stage 2 constituency with the depth of diversity in an inclusive, liberal constituency. As a rule, we can stipulate that the less uniformity there is in the stage 2 constituency, the fewer the demands action for such reasons places on members of the liberal constituency.

It will be objected here that the demandingness of justificatory reasons is irrelevant to the question of whether they are good reasons: for this, we assess them just according to moral ideals or the values of a true moral theory. However, my interest – as laid out in Chapter 1 – is in exploring the extent to which a theory of justificatory value which takes the motivational adequacy of justificatory reasons seriously can minimise the demandingness of these reasons without relinquishing their critical power. If a concern for motivational adequacy can be squared with a retention of critical power then we can have our cake and eat it, which in my view is a good thing.

Stage 2 should be read as a test of the motivational adequacy of stage 1 reasons, when motivational adequacy is understood in externalist or deliberative internalist terms. Wenar reads stage 2 as a test of motivational adequacy understood in sub-Humean terms, and so thinks that the fact that people as they are lack the motivational commitment to act for stage 1 justificatory reasons impugns the motivational adequacy of these reasons. That a deliberative internalist or externalist conception of motivational adequacy is required to escape criticisms like Wenar's means that Rawls' theory of justificatory values and reasons faces questions of demandingness. If Rawls is an externalist or a deliberative internalist with respect to justificatory reasons, then assessment of the motivational adequacy of these reasons *not only* requires an assessment of whether people could not reject them in the formal sense – i.e. without contradiction or inconsistency – *but also* an assessment of what it would take for these reasons to become motivating for people.

It is important to note here that an assessment of the demandingness of a reason does not involve assessing the probability that that reason will actually be accepted by people. Thus, my interest in the demandingness of justificatory reasons is not the same as Wenar's interest in the likelihood of their acceptance. A reason can be minimally demanding and yet be highly unlikely to be accepted by people as they are: perhaps existing political conditions and/or local traditions and customs which prevent the acceptance of a set of reasons exert such a strong hold over people that they are unlikely to escape this influence and accept the reasons in question. Alternatively, a set of reasons can be extremely demanding and yet be highly likely to be accepted: in George Orwell's *1984* propositions like '$2+2=5$' are likely to be accepted because the costs of not accepting them are so high.

The conception of the person at stage 2 clearly answers the formal question: it would be possible for people to accept stage 1 justificatory reasons without acquiring inconsistent beliefs or desires, so these reasons can be non-rejectable by these people. However, in order to assess the demandingness of Rawls' justificatory reasons we have to delve deeper, and examine how much uniformity is required among stage 2 people for these reasons to be non-rejectable by them. I shall argue that the demandingness of Rawls' justificatory reasons cannot be assessed until an ambiguity which runs deep in the heart of his conception of reasonableness, as modelled by the stage 2 ideal of the person, is cleared up. I shall discuss this in detail in section 2.4. Before doing that, let me outline Rawls' account of this ideal conception of the person, and the stage 1 justificatory reasons that this ideal tests for motivational adequacy.

2.3   Persons, society and value in ideal theory

Rawls constructs the values informing his stage 1 justificatory reasons from features of the ideal persons as he conceives of them at stage 2. I will not discuss all of these features in detail: let me first list these features before going on to say something brief about each one.

1. Persons have the capacity for a conception of the good.
2. Persons are reasonable:
   (a) they have the capacity for a sense of justice,
   (b) they accept the consequences of the burdens of judgement, and
   (c) they subscribe to a (full or partial) reasonable comprehensive doctrine.
3. Persons are rational.
4. Persons conceive of themselves as equal *qua* citizens.
5. Persons conceive of themselves as free *qua* citizens.
6. Persons value the conditions of their self-respect *qua* citizens.
7. Persons have a reasonable moral psychology.
8. Social co-operation is guided by publicly recognised rules which each person regards as appropriate and proper.

9. The terms of social co-operation are such that each person can reasonably accept them, so long as all others do.
10. Persons engaged in social co-operation have an idea of their own rational advantage.

Rawls thinks that each of these ideas is an idea of practical reason as it addresses questions of justice: 'we may call the conceptions of society and person "conceptions of practical reason": they characterize the agents who reason and questions to which principles of practical reason apply... Without conceptions of society and person, the principles of practical reason would have no point, use, or application.'[17] When Rawls claims that his conception of the person is an idea of practical reason he means that this conception provides the context in which practical reason is used to address the task of finding fair terms of social co-operation: 'conceptions of society and person characterize the agents who reason and specify the context of practical questions... We ask: what must persons be like to engage in practical reason?'[18] The idea is that unless we conceive of persons and their society as satisfying 1–10, we cannot conceive of them as being in a position to address questions of justice with practical reason at all.

1. *Persons have the capacity for a conception of the good*: This is 'the capacity to form, to revise, and rationally to pursue a conception of [their] rational advantage or good'.[19] Persons' conception of their own advantage will be informed by their conception of the good, which specifies what they take to be valuable in human life; what it means for persons to pursue this advantage rationally will be addressed below in (3).

2. Persons are reasonable, which means that,
   (a) *Persons possess the capacity for a sense of justice*. This is 'the capacity to understand, to apply, and to act from the public conception of justice which characterizes the fair terms of social cooperation... a sense of justice also expresses a willingness, if not the desire, to act in relation to others on terms that they can publicly endorse.'[20] When people have the capacity for a sense of justice they want to find publicly acceptable and mutually advantageous solutions to problems of social co-operation: they are not stubborn, manipulative, dishonest or perverse. The capacity for a sense of justice is one

of the two 'moral powers' that characterise persons in ideal theory. The other is the capacity for a conception of the good.

(b) *persons accept the consequences of the burdens of judgement* (I shall have more to say about this aspect of reasonableness shortly), and

(c) *persons subscribe to a (full or partial) reasonable comprehensive doctrine* which informs each of their conceptions of the good: 'We ... connect with ... a conception [of the good] a view of our relation to the world – religious, philosophical and moral – by reference to which the value and significance of our ends and attachments are understood'.[21]

3. *Persons are rational* in the pursuit of their conception of the good, that is, they adopt the most effective means to their ends and order these ends in a way that is meaningful given the comprehensive doctrine(s) informing their conception of the good (2c). Persons are rational when they pursue their ends by the most effective means, and order their ultimate ends in a way that has 'significance for their plan of life as a whole'.[22]

4. *Persons conceive of themselves as equal qua citizens* 'in virtue of possessing, to the requisite minimum degree, the two moral powers and other capacities that enable [them] to be normal and fully cooperating members of society'.[23]

5. *Persons conceive of themselves as free qua citizens*, by which is meant that each person,

(a) conceives of herself as having the right not to be identified with any particular conception of the good: 'as citizens, they are seen as capable of revising and changing [their conception of the good] on reasonable and rational grounds';[24]

(b) conceives of herself 'as [a] self-authenticating [source] of valid claims',[25] that is, as having the right to make claims on the political institutions of society to rationally advance her conception of the good, where these claims are conceived of as having weight just in virtue of being the claims of a person such as her;

(c) recognises that, 'the weight of [her] claims is not given by the strength and psychological intensity of [her] wants and desires (as opposed to [her] needs as citizens), even when [her] wants and desires are rational from [her] point of view'.[26] In this sense, persons take responsibility for their ends.

6. *Persons place value on the conditions of their self-respect qua citizens*, and thus they 'want to be, and to be recognized as [fully cooperating members of society]'.[27]

7. *Persons have a 'reasonable moral psychology'*, which means that they are moved by desires dependent on a conception of justice, are willing to act on these desires so long as other citizens do so too, and develop trust and confidence in other citizens when they act in this way, and trust and confidence in institutions when their fundamental interests in basic rights and liberties are protected by these institutions.[28]

Persons possessing features 1–8 at stage 2 are conceived of as accepting or rejecting principles of justice for society conceived of as 'a fair system of cooperation over time, from one generation to the next'.[29] This basic idea is to be cashed out in terms of three further ideas.

8. That '*[social] cooperation is guided by publicly recognized rules and procedures that those cooperating accept and regard as properly regulating their conduct*'.[30]

9. That the rules governing cooperation must be fair, where fairness is understood in terms of reciprocity such that *the terms of social cooperation are those that 'each participant may reasonably accept, provided that everyone else likewise accepts them'*.[31]

10. That *those engaged in social cooperation have an idea of their own rational advantage*, which 'specifies what those who are engaged in social cooperation … are trying to achieve, when the scheme is viewed from their own standpoint'.[32]

This inventory of the ideas involved in stage 2 of justification bears out the truth of Rawls' claim that his Constructivism 'uses a rather complex conception of the person and society to give form and structure to its construction'.[33] These conceptions of the person and society are justified in a distinctively Constructivist way on the grounds that unless persons and society are conceived in this way, persons cannot be thought of as solving problems of justice through the use of their practical reason. Instead, persons would have to be thought of as relying on an external authority to solve these problems for them; but given deep diversity, we cannot assume that persons agree upon such an authority.[34]

In section 2.4 I shall disambiguate three different readings of (2b) (acceptance of the consequences of the burdens of judgement) and argue that one of these readings is less demanding than the other two, and yet still allows that stage 1 justificatory reasons could not be rejected by stage 2 persons. In the next two chapters I will argue that by exploiting the resources available in (6) (a conception of the person as valuing her self-respect and its social bases) we can reject (2b) as part of the ideal of the person without a loss of critical power in justificatory reasons: these chapters aim to show how we can have our cake and eat it.

Let me pause here to discuss in some more detail the important idea of the burdens of judgement (2b), which explains, for Rawls, why even a well-ordered society is ineradicably diverse. My discussion here will be limited just to exposition and rejection of some misinterpretations: discussion of the ambiguity with respect to the burdens of judgement will come later.

It might be thought that rational people seeking a mutually acceptable agreement among themselves to the problem of social justice would come to actively share a set of values, ends or beliefs from which principles of justice could be derived. However, Rawls claims that this assumption should not form part of a theory of justificatory value. His explanation of why not is in his account of the burdens of judgement, which explain the persistence of disagreement between ideally rational and reasonable people on matters involving the use of their judgement.

The burdens of judgement are that:

a. 'The evidence – empirical and scientific – bearing on the case is conflicting and complex, and thus hard to assess and evaluate'.
b. Agreement on the considerations relevant to a particular judgement does not guarantee agreement with respect to how these considerations should be weighted in judgement.
c. The concepts appearing in judgement 'are vague and subject to hard cases', making interpretation unavoidable.
d. 'To some extent … the way we assess evidence and weigh moral and political values is shaped by our total experience, our whole course of life up till now: and our total experiences must always differ'.
e. Normative considerations in cases of judgement are hard to assess, both on their own, and in relation to one another when they are in competition.
f. '[A]ny system of institutions has, as it were, a limited social space'. In the same way that a person cannot guarantee the realisation of

everything she values in her own life, given the practical restrictions that a limited life span places on the number of ends and plans that a person can pursue, so political institutions cannot be guaranteed to protect all our 'cherished values'. We find choices between these values hard to make precisely because they are deeply cherished, and disagreement among reasonable people on which value is to be prioritised is inevitable.[35]

The burdens of judgement explain why rational people committed to finding publicly acceptable principles of justice, and with the best will in the world, cannot be expected to come to unanimous, or even near unanimous, agreement on important matters involving the use of judgement.

It is important to note that Rawls is not making any of the following sceptical claims: (1) that there is no truth of the matter with respect to disagreements involving judgement; (2) that the truth of the matter with respect to disagreements involving judgement can never be known; or (3) that persons ought to have a sceptical attitude towards their own beliefs in virtue of the fact that they cannot convince others to share them.[36] The burdens of judgement only explain why reasonable and rational people cannot be expected to agree in matters of judgement, and have no implications for the fact of the matter, if there is one, with respect to these disagreements, or for the attitude that persons ought to have towards their own beliefs.

Accepting that reasonable pluralism is the outcome of the exercise of human reason in conditions of freedom, must we agree with Rawls that this fact of human life is not to be regretted?[37] One way of disagreeing with Rawls would be to claim that although reasonable pluralism is indeed the inevitable outcome of the free exercise of human reason, this is because human beings are flawed and prone to error, and this fact is to be regretted. A suggestion along these lines is made by David Estlund when he claims that '[in] order to avoid relying on the strong skeptical views either that there is no truth on [matters of judgement] or that even if there is truth there is no knowledge of it, one must explain disagreement as an *epistemic failure* of at least some people to know things that may be knowable'.[38]

Estlund's argument has the following structure: if commitment to the burdens of judgement is to avoid the implication that (1) there is no truth of the matter with respect to disagreements involving judgement, or (2) the truth of these matters can never be known, then commitment to the burdens of judgement must imply that (1) there are truths of the matter with respect to disagreements involving judgement, or (2) the truth of these matters can be known. But this argument is flawed. That Rawls claims that the burdens of judgement do not entail either of the sceptical claims does not entail that in asserting the burdens of judgement he is committed to the negation of either or both of the sceptical claims. Rawls' claim is not that the burdens of judgement do not entail scepticism because they entail non-scepticism; rather, Rawls' claim is that the burdens of judgement have no implications for scepticism, or any other position on the existence of truths and their knowability. In which case, we need not view the disagreement made inevitable by the burdens of judgement in terms of regrettable epistemic failure.[39]

What are the consequences of acceptance of the burdens of judgement? Rawls claims that their acceptance means that not all forms of pluralism can be explained in terms of the irrationality, stubbornness or stupidity of those who hold diverse views: some forms of pluralism are reasonable, and therefore not to be regretted as a side-effect of epistemic failure.[40] We cannot assume that disagreement on matters requiring the use of judgement will disappear, even in the best of conditions. Rawls' emphasis, in *Political Liberalism*, on the enduring fact of reasonable pluralism as explained by the burdens of judgement marks, he thinks, the key difference between the ideal theory of *Political Liberalism* and the ideal theory of *A Theory of Justice*. In Part III of *A Theory of Justice* Rawls thinks that he made assumptions that conflict with acceptance of the permanent fact of reasonable pluralism: here, rational and reasonable persons are characterised as sharing a set of ends understood in terms of a broadly Kantian conception of the good. In *Political Liberalism* Rawls' aim is to address questions of political justification in an ideal theory allowing for greater diversity among reasonable and rational people.[41]

Rawls thinks that acceptance of the consequences of the burdens of judgement has two important implications for the principles and procedures justified by stage 1 values and reasons. These relate to political toleration, and to public reason.

Toleration

If a reasonable person realises that she and all other reasonable people are under the burdens of judgement then, when other reasonable people disagree with her, she does not conclude that these people are stupid, wilful, obstructive or misinformed, even though she thinks that these people have false beliefs with respect to the issue over which they disagree, given that for her to believe something is for her to believe it to be true. In a society characterised by inevitable reasonable disagreement, and mutual acceptance of the burdens of judgement, a reasonable person realises that, however convinced she is of the truth of her own views, to insist that political principles be based on these views in virtue of their truth appears to other people, with different reasonable views, to be an insistence that her views have this importance simply because they are *her* views.[42] So a reasonable person will refrain from using state power to enforce her preferred political principles on others with equally reasonable views: reasonable people who accept the consequences of the burdens of judgement endorse political principles of toleration.[43]

Public reason

Given that the political decisions of reasonable people are not made by reference to the truth of views over which there is reasonable disagreement, how do such people make these decisions? There are actually two questions here: (a) how do reasonable people come to agree upon 'substantive principles of justice for the basic structure' of society?; (b) what 'guidelines of inquiry' do reasonable people adopt 'to decide whether substantive principles properly apply and to identify laws and policies that best satisfy them'?[44] In both cases Rawls claims that ideal citizens debate their decisions in public reason, that is, in terms of reasons which they take to be acceptable to other reasonable – and possibly very different – people.[45] Ideal citizens accept the possibility that others will differ from them without concluding that this difference shows that others are unreasonable, and this is the case because they accept the burdens of judgement.

By adopting procedures governed by the 'ideal of public reason', Rawls thinks that reasonable people can reach consensus on principles of justice. Given that a person accepts the fact of reasonable pluralism, if she simply asserts her own comprehensive views about the correct solution to problems of justice as decisive, she does not offer others reasons fit to justify her proposals *to them*. As Rawls remarks, 'public justification is not simply valid reasoning, but argument *addressed to others*'.[46] If reasonable pluralism is permanent, all persons accept this by accepting the burdens of judgement, and all persons are assumed to have the capacity for a sense of justice, then no person can expect all reasonable others to have reasons for supporting certain principles of justice which are identical to her own. Accepting the fact of reasonable pluralism means accepting that the free exercise of reason creates a plurality of comprehensive views about justice, and other matters, and thus that reasonable people cannot be expected to reach agreement on comprehensive matters. In that case, any reasonable person engaged in justificatory debate must offer others justificatory reasons which she sincerely and genuinely takes to be reasons that others could accept as justificatory reasons through the free use of their reason, given their willingness to propose and abide by fair principles of justice. For Rawls, the ideal of public reason in procedural justice is captured by the following three conditions.[47]

(1) Public officials – judges, legislators, candidates for public office etc. – present their political justifications to citizens in terms of reasons which they sincerely and genuinely take to be reasons which the public, and other officials, could endorse through the use of their reason.[48]

(2) Ordinary citizens 'view themselves as ideal legislators' in order to judge whether public officials satisfy (1), and do what they can to criticise and remove from office public officials who fail to satisfy (1).[49]

(3) Ordinary citizens are willing and able to offer to one another only those justificatory reasons which they sincerely and genuinely take to be reasons that each could accept as justificatory reasons through the use of their reason, given their acceptance of the burdens of judgement, which means that they will permanently differ with respect to questions involving the use of judgement.[50]

The stage 1 conception of justice which Rawls thinks could not be rejected by stage 2 people is articulated in terms of public reason, toleration and the values of political justice. Let me outline Rawls' argument.

Any stage 2 person will know that she differs on fundamental matters of judgement from others who are just as reasonable as she is (2b and 2c). But she knows that these others are also motivated to find principles of justice (2a), and she knows that these people care, as she does, that their rational advantage is well represented by whatever principles are agreed upon (10). These aspects of stage 2 people partly explain why they can only accept principles of justice which state reasons for their acceptance that each reasonable person can accept, given that other reasonable people do so as well (9). In such a society reasonable people cannot accept a conception of justice stating reasons for its acceptance which are only indexed to, and just expressed in terms of, a particular moral, religious or philosophical comprehensive doctrine that could be subscribed to by a reasonable person. Instead, the reasons stated by this conception must provide 'a publicly recognized point of view from which all citizens can examine before one another whether their political and social institutions are just'.[51] This is the case both with respect to the reasons given for accepting principles to govern the basic structure of society, and with respect to the reasons citizens offer to one another when enquiring about how principles of justice ought to shape their social institutions.[52] One way of expressing this idea is to say that a stage 1 conception of justice must be epistemically abstinent with respect to comprehensive moral, religious and philosophical matters.[53]

What values must inform a stage 1 conception of justice stating public reasons for its acceptance? Rawls claims that these values of political justice are: 'equal political and civil liberty; equality of opportunity; the values of social equality and economic reciprocity; and … values of the common good as well as the various necessary conditions for all these values'.[54] The task of showing how a conception of justice informed by these values is acceptable to stage 2 people was started by Rawls in Parts I and II of *A Theory of Justice*, continued in Part III *Political Liberalism*, and still continues in recent pieces such as *Justice as Fairness: A Restatement*.[55] Some of these arguments will be addressed later in Chapter 5 when I examine the political implications of treating self-respect as a justificatory value.

This is, in outline, Rawls' Constructivist approach to justice-justification. In the next two sections I shall address worries about the demandingness aspect of motivational adequacy as they arise for Rawls' Constructivism. The argument will be that Rawls' characterisation of persons as accepting the consequences of the burdens of judgement (2b) is ambiguous between three interpretations. On two of these readings, justificatory reasons appear worryingly demanding, but on the alternative less demanding reading, it is left unclear why ideal persons could not reject reasons to practice toleration and endorse public reason. However, unless there are grounds for claiming that persons facing problems of justice *qua* practical reasoners could not reject toleration and public reason, the critical potential of Rawlsian justificatory reasons is lost. If we advocate the least demanding reading of (2b) then we must provide alternative grounds for thinking that persons *qua* justice-seeking practical reasoners could not reject reasons to practice toleration and endorse public reason. These alternative grounds are laid out in the next two chapters, where I offer an account of self-respect as the context for justice-oriented practical reasoning. I shall argue that – holding all other aspects of the stage 2 conception of the person constant – persons in ideal theory ought to be thought of as caring about the social bases of their self-respect, and accepting that all others do so too, and that this provides the grounds for thinking that justice-seeking practical reasoners could not reject reasons to practice toleration and endorse public reason. If less demanding reasons are preferable to more demanding reasons then – all else being equal – we should prefer a self-respect based liberal Constructivism to a Constructivism based on the burdens of judgement. Or so I shall argue.

2.4   The burdens of judgement, motivational adequacy and demandingness

When we ask whether ideal persons at stage 2 could not reject stage 1 justificatory reasons we are in part testing whether acceptance of these reasons requires action for contradictory reasons or inconsistent motives.[56] On my view, however, not only should we test these reasons according to formal criteria; we should also treat stage 2 as a test of the demandingness of these reasons. With respect to stage 1 reasons which are formally acceptable to stage 2 people, we need to ask: what would it take for these reasons to become motivating for members of a deeply diverse and inclusive constituency of justification? Or, what would it take for people in such a constituency to become stage 2 people? The demandingness of stage 1 reasons can be assessed by examining how much uniformity has to be assumed among stage 2 people before we can confidently claim that they could all be motivated to act according to the stage 1 reasons which they could not reject: the more uniformity we have to assume, the greater the demandingness of the reasons.

There are ambiguities in one key aspect of Rawls' conception of the person which leaves it unclear how much uniformity is built into this conception, and thus unclear how demanding his stage 1 justificatory reasons really are. This ambiguity attaches to his claim that stage 2 people accept the consequences of the burdens of judgement. By clearing up the ambiguity we will see that Rawls' account of stage 2 persons as accepting the burdens of judgement makes his stage 1 reasons appear more demanding than they have to be. I shall argue that an account of why ideal people accept the permanence of pluralism can be given which does not rely on specifying that they accept the burdens of judgement. The problem with this account is that it leaves Constructivism without a motivational story to explain why stage 2 people could all be motivated by stage 1 reasons to practice toleration and exercise public reason when they cannot be assumed to view their disagreements as reasonable. In the next two chapters I shall present such a motivational story which is consistent with – indeed, suggested by – many remarks Rawls makes about how ideal people care about their self-respect and its social conditions. Once we assume that ideal people are oriented towards their self-respect, an account of its social conditions shows that stage 1 reasons could become motivating for stage 2 people, which means that we can ditch the assumption that these ideal people all share the same beliefs about why pluralism is permanent. The big advantage of this account is that it makes stage 1 reasons less demanding than on Rawls' account, and yet retains the critical power of Rawls' two-stage Constructivist procedure by preserving the emphasis – at both stages – on the reasons people *could not reject,* rather than those they are likely to accept. The account remains fully normative, but is more suited to justification to an inclusive, deeply diverse constituency than Rawls' account because its reasons are less demanding. To see how all of this works we must first address the ambiguities in Rawls' account.

I will distinguish two different ways of understanding the following claim: the fact that reason operates under burdens explains why pluralism is permanent. The demandingness of each of these interpretations can then be tested by asking how much uniformity must be assumed across people for it to be possible for justificatory reasons constructed against the background of each of these interpretations to become motivating for them.

The first interpretation is that pluralism is permanent because reason underdetermines belief, especially beliefs about values. Call this the 'underdetermination' view. The view is that reason has limits, and once these limits are reached, the paths to belief are diverse and no longer track the demands of reason. Thus, once the limits of reason have been reached, pluralism is reasonable, because all belief sets within pluralism are consistent with reason, even though none of them is demanded by reason. With respect to (at least) beliefs about value, reason runs out without uniquely specifying any one set of beliefs. Beyond reason, belief sets vary according to the demands of faith, habit, upbringing and other paths to belief which do not track reason. The underdetermination view can be pictured as in Figure 2.1.

In 'Justice as Fairness: Political not Metaphysical' – a paper which is an important prelude to *Political Liberalism*, and is recast in large

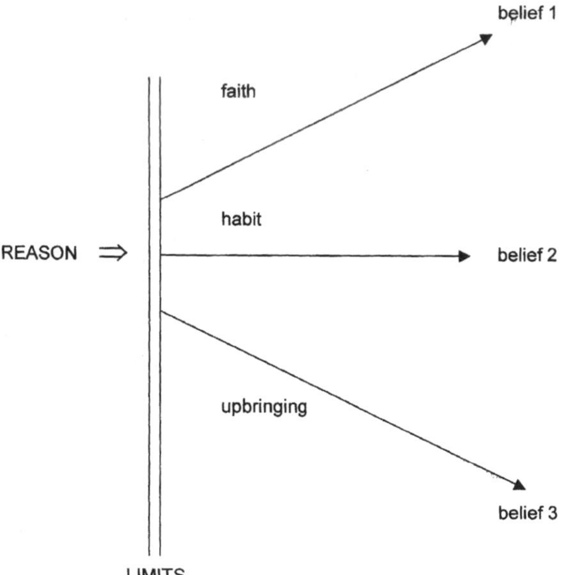

Figure 2.1   The 'underdetermination' view

part in that book – Rawls appears to endorse the underdetermination view of the burdens of judgement.

> [L]iberalism as a political doctrine supposes that there are many conflicting and incommensurable conceptions of the good, each compatible with the full rationality of human persons… As a consequence of this supposition, liberalism assumes that it is a characteristic feature of a free democratic culture that a plurality of conflicting and incommensurable conceptions of the good are affirmed by its citizens.[57]

In this passage Rawls explains the permanent fact of pluralism by reference to the incommensurability of peoples' conceptions of the good, even in the best of conditions. This means that conceptions of the good cannot be ranked according to a master value, or ranked by comparison with one another. This can be seen as a version of the underdetermination view because once reason reaches its limits it can specify no value according to which different conceptions of the good can be ranked, and neither can it guide comparisons of conceptions of the good in the absence of a master-value. There are many accounts of incommensurability in the literature, and not all of them cast incommensurability in terms of the underdetermination of beliefs about value by reason.[58] But this is how incommensurability must be cast if it provides the key to understanding why the operation of reason makes pluralism a permanent fact, and it is this that we are trying to understand by looking at Rawls.

There are two problems with the underdetermination view. First, I have argued elsewhere that imputing to ideal people a belief in the incommensurability of conceptions of the good has no consequences for whether stage 1 reasons to practice toleration are motivationally adequate for these ideal people. Incommensurability is a view about the *nature* of pluralism, whereas the motivation to practice toleration must respond to beliefs about the *character* of pluralism. With respect to the character of pluralism, theses of incommensurability remain silent: the truth or falsity of theses of incommensurability is simply irrelevant to the question of whether principles of toleration are justified.[59]

More germane to my topic here, however, is a problem with the demandingness of the underdetermination view. On this account, we must assume that stage 2 people believe that reason runs out before any one set of beliefs about value is specified as uniquely reasonable. This belief entails a belief that reasonable pluralism is permanent. So, for ideal people to be motivated by stage 1 reasons to practice toleration (ignoring the criticism above) and to endorse public reason requires that they all believe:

(a) that different belief sets ought not to be subject to criticism through the use of reason, because their incommensurability means that they cannot be ranked against one another through the use of reason; and that,

(b) as a consequence, reasonable pluralism is a permanent fact.

The worry about the underdetermination view is the demandingness of (a). Theses of incommensurability are highly controversial. To require that all people accept the truth of these theses – that all people become uniform in their beliefs about the limitations of reason – is very demanding. But according to the underdetermination view, stage 2 people not only agree that reason has limits. According to this view, they also agree about what these limits are; that is, they agree about the point at which reason runs out with respect to beliefs about value. Again, this is deeply controversial, even among philosophers who accept theses of incommensurability in principle. Given these problems, is there a less demanding interpretation of the connection between the burdens of reason and the permanence of pluralism?

The second reading of this connection is suggested by something striking in Rawls' recasting of 'Justice as Fairness: Political not Metaphysical' in Lecture I of *Political Liberalism*.[60] Here, all reference to incommensurability as the consequence of reason's burdened operation is removed. Instead, in Lecture II, we get an account of the permanence of pluralism in terms of the six burdens of judgement listed on p. 39, none of which make mention of incommensurability. Instead, pluralism is claimed to be permanent because burdened reason operating in conditions of freedom prevents convergence on beliefs (especially beliefs about values). Let me call this the 'burdens of judgement' reading (or the 'burdens' reading, for short). We can represent this reading as in Figure 2.2.

On the burdens reading, stage 2 people accept that pluralism is permanent *because* they believe that the exercise of judgement is subject

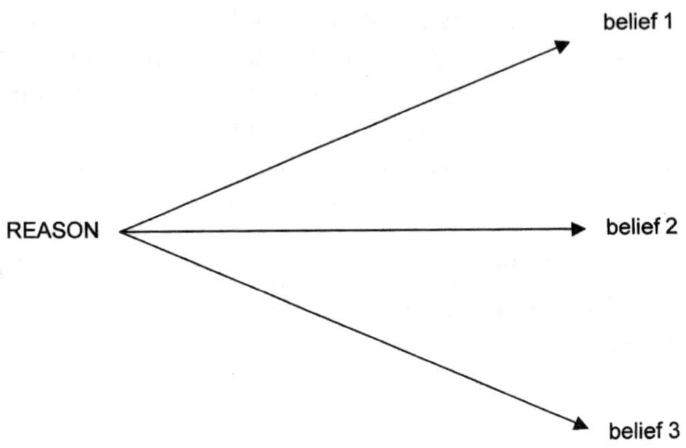

Figure 2.2   The 'burdens' view

to certain burdens which make disagreement inevitable even in ideal conditions: they all accept the same explanation of why they cannot expect to convince one another of their views through the exercise of reason, even in the best of conditions. In that case, people who recognise these burdens of judgement accept that reasonable pluralism is ineradicable. There are lots of places in *Political Liberalism* where Rawls endorses the burdens view. For example,

> [R]easonable persons … recognize that all persons alike, including themselves, are subject to [the burdens of judgement], and so many reasonable comprehensive doctrines are affirmed, not all of which can be true (indeed none of them may be true).[61]

The burdens view is less demanding than the underdetermination view because the beliefs it requires that people come to acquire in order for it to be possible for them to be motivated by justificatory reasons are less controversial than the theses of incommensurability. For example, that 'the evidence – empirical and scientific – bearing on [any] case is conflicting and complex, and thus hard to assess and evaluate',[62] and that, 'To some extent … the way we assess evidence and weigh moral and political values is shaped by our total experience, our whole course of life up till now: and our total experience must always differ'.[63] These are statements that many people with different beliefs could come to share without relinquishing these beliefs. Nevertheless, once we pick apart the burdens view it becomes clear that the demands it makes are not insubstantial.

On the burdens view each person must accept the same explanation of the permanence of pluralism, and accept that this explanation applies not just to others, but also to herself. Given that acceptance of an explanation involves the acquisition of beliefs, the burdens view – like the underdetermination view – demands some uniformity of belief with respect to the sources of pluralism. The thought behind the burdens view is that it is only if people accept pluralism as permanent in virtue of the fact that everyone stands under the burdens of judgement that people will restrain themselves with respect to the use of power to suppress the view of others – i.e., practice toleration – and present their political reasons to others in terms they take to be acceptable to them (i.e., be committed to public reason). The burdens view is supposed to ensure that persons' acceptance of stage 1 principles and procedures goes beyond *modus vivendi*.

But consider what the burdens view asks of each person in conditions of pluralism: each person must explain her disagreement with others in terms of the fact that all persons are subject to the burdens of judgement. This means that she must accept that she too stands under these burdens. *Pace* Brian Barry, this does not mean that she should be sceptical about the truth of her own beliefs, or water down her commitment to them.[64] But it does mean that – even in the face of her total conviction of their truth and dedicated commitment to a life lived according to them – she must accept that, even in ideal circumstances when everyone else exercises their judgement carefully and correctly, she cannot expect to convince others of her beliefs.

On the burdens view, all persons accept this fact about the way in which they and others exercise their judgement. The problem with the burdens view is the demandingness of this requirement. When we think of people who might deny that the burdens of judgement apply to them, it is tempting to think just of fervent devotees or political true believers who assume their own infallibility and so cannot accept that they could not convince others of their beliefs in ideal conditions, i.e. conditions in which these others exercise their judgement correctly. Of course, reasons to practice toleration and endorse public reason will not be motivating for such people, if being motivated to act for these reasons requires acceptance of the burdens under which one's own judgement operates. But the burdens view is demanding not just for true believers, but also for common or garden believers who do not burn with the fire of conviction, but would nevertheless be hard pushed to accept that their judgement as it addresses pedestrian matters is burdened. Mundane believers must accept that, even in ideal conditions when everyone exercises their judgement correctly and carefully, they cannot expect to convince flat-earthers that the earth is round, South Sea Islanders that Prince Philip is not a god, or Russell's interlocutor that it is not turtles all the way down.[65] It may be the case that in deep diversity many people do accept that the judgements which ground many of their beliefs are subject to burdens. But to insist that all persons accept this with respect to the exercise of their judgement *per se* seems very demanding, especially if there is an alternative way to conceive of stage 2 persons that yields the same results with respect to justificatory reasons, i.e. that stage 2 persons could be motivated by stage 1 reasons to practice toleration and endorse public reason. Justificatory reasons premised on the burdens view will not speak to persons whose commitment to their beliefs and values – regardless of their content – makes no room for the thought that their own judgement is subject to burdens. The account of the grounds on which stage 2 people find stage 1 reasons non-rejectable à la the burdens view means that these reasons could be rejected by people who reject the burdens of judgement. If such people – who, crucially, may possess all the other characteristics of stage 2 persons – are excluded from the constituency of justification then liberals had better have a good reason for this exclusion.

The hard-nosed response here will be to insist that the burdens view is a proper part of the ideal conception of reasonableness, and that people who fail to conform to the expectations which issue from it simply fail to be reasonable. The response will be that the fact that a person finds it very difficult to radically revise her existing beliefs in order to become motivated by justificatory reasons says much about what is wrong with this person and nothing about what is wrong with the justification in which the reasons appear.

The insight in this response is that all political justifications operating with externalist or deliberative internalist criteria of motivational adequacy demand *something* of those in the constituency of justification; a political justification which lacked any demands would be one which lacked critical distance. But note that what is problematical here is that what is being demanded will be difficult to acquire *across the board of comprehensive views*. The worry is not that some persons are being excluded in virtue of, say, their racist or sexist beliefs: critically potent liberal justifications rightly demand that these beliefs are not expressed in political reasons. Rather, the worry is that any person who denies that the judgement upon which her commitment to her beliefs and values rests is burdened – *whatever these beliefs and values are*, however trivial or mundane – may be excluded from the constituency of justification just in virtue of this denial. If only a conception of one's own judgement as burdened can bring commitment to toleration and public reason, then liberal Constructivist justification is in danger of preaching to the converted.

Is there a less demanding account of the permanence of pluralism which nevertheless explains why reasons for practising toleration and engaging in public reason could be motivating for stage 2 people? The final account I shall consider eschews appeal to theses of incommensurability or the burdens of judgement. Instead, this account allows that people will differ with respect to their explanations of why pluralism is a permanent fact, just as they differ in the paths they take to their most cherished and important beliefs. On this view, all persons recognise the practical impossibility of reaching agreement with respect to the truth of various comprehensive doctrines, but they do not unite on an explanation of why this is impossible. On this view, persons are as divided with respect to the explanation of the fact of pluralism as they are with respect to moral, religious and philosophical questions, and how they arrive at their answers to them. Some people will acquire their beliefs through faith; for them, the permanence of pluralism might be explained by God's inscrutable plan for his creatures. Others will claim that their beliefs are informed by reason; for them, the permanence of pluralism might be explained by the epistemic failure of human beings. Yet others may acquire their beliefs through reflective endorsement of the tradition of thought into which they were born; for them, permanent pluralism may be explained by an incommensurability thesis. Let me call this the 'many flowers' view.

On the many flowers view, the expectation is not that persons agree upon one explanation of the permanence of pluralism. Different people will explain the permanence of deep diversity in terms of scepticism, epistemic failure, human laziness, mass ignorance, etc. This creates a worry about the many flowers view: unless a person conceives of pluralism as (at least potentially) reasonable through acceptance of the burdens of judgement, her commitment to the permanence of pluralism will not be genuine. The fear is that unless we assume that persons accept the permanence of pluralism *as a consequence of* the proper exercise of reason itself, then we cannot assume that, should the balance of power between them and those with whom they disagree change, they will not attempt to use this power to correct, or just suppress, those who disagree with them. Without uniformity of belief here, uniformity of motivation with respect to toleration and public reason are not secured.

Are these worries about the many flowers view well placed? Should we think that, for example, a person who explains the permanence of pluralism in terms of scepticism, the epistemic failure of others, or the laziness of others, will in virtue of these beliefs be less motivationally committed to the practice of toleration and public reason than a person who recognises the burdens of judgement, or accepts incommensurability, given that the person *genuinely* accepts that pluralism is a permanent fact? Much hangs on what is involved in a person genuinely accepting that pluralism is a permanent fact. The many flowers view must, I think, make at least this demand of people: that they acknowledge that whenever conditions of freedom have obtained in the past, beliefs about moral, religious and philosophical questions have diverged. The many flowers view means that people who accept this fact about human history will differ with respect to what makes it a fact. However, to be sure that they do not retain a secret glimmering vision of a world united behind their own beliefs, we must ask them to take the record of history seriously. This is a demand, but it is not one that discriminates between different philosophical accounts of pluralism (as the underdetermination view does), and neither does it require uniformity with respect to the way in which people conceive of the operation of their own understanding (as the burdens view does).

However, the many flowers view still needs more by way of a story about why stage 2 persons are motivationally committed to toleration and public reason. These persons may take the record of history very seriously; what they learn from it may be that they can never expect to convince *everyone* of their views, with reason, coercion or revelation. But they may nevertheless believe that these means can be used to convince a large part of humanity, and they may believe that that part is the membership of their constituency of justification.

In that case, although their acceptance of the record of history may prevent them from undertaking world crusades or a global Inquisition, it need not prevent them from aiming at state totalitarianism, which is hardly what we would call tolerant.

If the many flowers view is to stand as an account of how stage 1 reasons could motivate stage 2 people *and* be less demanding than the alternative views, then it must explain why people divided on the question of why pluralism is a permanent fact are all nevertheless committed to toleration and public reason. In the next two chapters I shall develop an account of self-respect and its social conditions which, I believe, provides the missing part of the motivational story needed to support the many flowers view. This view, with the account to be developed in the next two chapters, can be represented as shown in Figure 2.3.

In brief, I shall argue that, regardless of the differences in their paths to self-respect, stage 2 people should be thought of as motivationally uniform with respect to their self-respect. Diverse beliefs acquired through diverse means – reason, faith, habit, upbringing etc. – can all supply the personal bases of self-respect. Given this uniformity of motivation, I shall argue that the social contexts in which self-respect is developed – the dynamics of close associational life and citizenship – explain why people deeply divided in their beliefs and paths to them could be motivated to practice toleration and endorse public reason.

This chapter has given an account of Rawls' Constructivism and suggested three explanations of why the ideal persons of this procedure

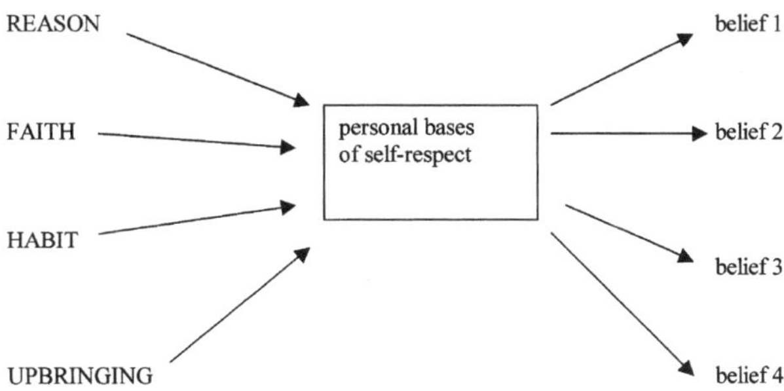

Figure 2.3 The 'many flowers' view

of justification should be thought of as accepting the permanence of pluralism, and as being committed to the practice of toleration and the engagement in public reason in virtue of this acceptance. I have suggested that the underdetermination and burdens interpretations of this feature of ideal persons are more demanding than the many flowers view, which turns on the idea that persons are committed to their self-respect and its social conditions. In order to support this suggestion I shall, in the next chapter, give an account of self-respect and its social conditions. In Chapter 4 I address the question of how conceiving of persons as caring about their self-respect and its social conditions makes it possible for them to be motivated by reasons to practice toleration and endorse public reason.

3
Self-Respect

3.1   Introduction

In this chapter I shall give an account of self-respect as a justificatory value for the Constructivist approach sketched at the end of the last chapter. My claim there was that by placing more emphasis on self-respect in the ideal of the person appearing at stage 2 of political justification, the problems of demandingness thrown up by the incommensurability and the burdens interpretations of acceptance of the permanence of pluralism can be avoided. In this chapter and the next I develop an account of self-respect and its role in practical reasoning about problems of justice, and I offer an account of the social conditions in which self-respect is normally developed which draws on ideas in Rawls. These accounts fill the motivational gap in the many flowers view laid out at the end of the last chapter: they show why people who believe that pluralism is permanent because of the diverse ways in which self-respect can be developed could not reject reasons to practice toleration and engage in public reason.

3.2   Self-respect: standards and success

Let me start my characterisation of self-respect with an intuitive thought: a person's self-respect depends on her being or striving to be the kind of person she wants to be. A person's self-respect requires congruence between her self-conception and her self-expression; it depends upon her meeting standards with which she in some way identifies. Self-respect requires that a person act in ways at least consistent with and preferably supportive of her self-conception. In failing to act in these ways a person fails to be as she had thought she was or hoped she could be.

Each person's self-conception carries with it standards of excellence for the activities which inform that self-conception. For example, if a person conceives of herself as a teacher then the standards by which she judges herself successful as a teacher might make reference to the patience, sensitivity and administrative skills she brings to her teaching. Alternatively, if a person's self-conception revolves around Christian ideals then the standards implicit in her self-conception might make reference to the charity, benevolence and self-control in the face of temptation which she exhibits across the whole range of her life activities. Or, if a person conceives of herself as an artist then perhaps the relevant standards will make reference to creativity, intellectual independence and artistic integrity. Achieving the congruence that matters for self-respect requires that a person judge herself successful according to standards of excellence implicit in her self-conception.

There are at least two ways in which this success can be understood; each of these understandings has different implications for the nature of self-respect.

One straightforward way in which a person can achieve congruence is by meeting social criteria for the activities she values. This is the kind of success Nozick has in mind in the following examples:

> A man living in a isolated mountain village can sink 15 jump shots with a basket ball out of 150 tries. Everyone else in the village can sink only 1 jump shot out of 150 tries. He thinks (as do the others) that he's very good at it. One day, along comes Jerry West. Or, a mathematician works very hard and occasionally thinks up an interesting conjecture, nicely proves a theorem, and so on. He then discovers a whole group of whizzes at mathematics. He dreams up a conjecture, and they quickly prove or disprove it (not in all possible cases, because of Church's theorem), constructing very elegant proofs; they themselves also think up deep theorems, and so on.[1]

In Nozick's examples a person measures her success at activities she values using the criteria of success employed by her community.

Social criteria of excellence are standards employed by communities or groups to set goals for, distribute rewards to,[2] and provide incentives for their members. Hence, the existence of social criteria of excellence in a group at a given time depends on a degree of consensus within that group with respect to 'the ideal form' of that to which the criteria apply, and consensus on this ideal form can change when the community encounters new and better ways of pursuing the activities to which the criteria apply.

Nozick asserts that 'There is no standard of doing something well, independent of how it is or can be done by others.'[3] Should we conceive of self-respect in terms of success according to social criteria of excellence?[4] Is an undeniable failure according to social criteria of excellence sufficient to undermine a person's self-respect? It is clear that such failure will have an effect on the self-respect of *some* people. Those who define themselves according to roles and values upheld by their community will receive a shock to their self-conceptions upon failing according to the very standards that they themselves endorse. But this suggests that what matters for self-respect is not the (social or non-social) origins of standards of excellence themselves, but rather the extent to which a person identifies with these standards. Focusing just on social criteria of excellence obscures this important point. We do better in explaining the standards relevant to self-respect by examining their relationship with a person's self-conception.

A better way to understand the congruence that matters for self-respect, then, is by analysing it in terms of success according to what I shall call 'individual criteria of excellence'. Individual criteria of excellence relate to a person's conception of her 'ideal self'. This is not a person's conception of what she would be like were the world a perfect place and she had all the talents, abilities and social successes she could wish for, but rather a conception of what she can achieve – of what is possible for her – given her own particular and actual talents and abilities. For example, a place in the chorus of a local amateur opera company would not normally qualify a person as a great diva according to social criteria of excellence for singers. But a person might, notwithstanding her poor performance according to social criteria, view herself as having achieved something according to her own lights, given the knowledge she has of her particular limitations.[5] It is clear that, *pace* Nozick, success can have both a social and a more private aspect; it is the latter kind of success that ultimately matters for self-respect. The attempt here is not to set up individual standards in opposition to social standards. To the contrary, it can be – and probably is – true that most people's individual criteria of excellence are partially informed by or are identical to social criteria. The point is just that it is the fact that a person identifies herself with these standards that makes them relevant to her self-respect, not the fact that others with whom she associates judge success or failure according to these standards.

The content and the stringency of individual criteria of excellence will depend on the talents and abilities of the person whose standards they are, and may well look poor when compared to relevantly similar social criteria used by individuals in a group to compare their performance to others in that group. Alternatively, individual criteria may be identical to, or even more demanding than, counterpart social criteria. The latter is the case with perfectionists who eschew social standards in favour of their own, sometimes impossible, goals. However, the point about individual criteria is that, insofar as they relate to self-respect, they are relativised to the person whose criteria they are. Thus, the public mediocrity of Nozick's disappointed basketball player and his eclipsed mathematician need not undermine their self-respect, so long as they succeed according to their own lights. Furthermore, this conception makes self-respect a matter of degree, because a person can be more or less successful in meeting the criteria of excellence which relate to her self-respect.

It might be objected that the distinction between individual and social criteria is untenable. To possess individual criteria of excellence for activity Φ a person must have been involved in Φ-ing at least once. If this were not the case then it would be impossible for a person to form such criteria, because she would have no idea of her limitations and talents with respect to Φ, and thus have no way of determining subjective standards of excellence for herself. If possession of individual criteria of excellence requires some involvement in the activity to which they relate then it seems impossible for a person who has never attempted Φ to have an idea of what it would be to be good at Φ. For example, a childless man could have no idea of what it is to be a good parent. But this is patently false. Thus the distinction between social and individual criteria of excellence should be abandoned. All criteria of excellence are social criteria.

This objection rests on a misunderstanding of the distinction, which does not entail, for example, that a childless man cannot have a conception of what it would be to be a good parent, but only that he cannot, all else being equal, have a conception of what it would be for *him* to be a good parent, and this latter kind of conception is what matters for self-respect. A childless man can have a conception of good parenting simply by consulting some set of pre-established social criteria of excellence for child rearing. Such criteria are characterised by their ready availability for consultation, their accessibility to all: they are fully public. But they are distinct from individual criteria which a person cannot form unless she has engaged in the activity to which they relate at least once.

One worry about this characterisation of individual criteria of excellence is that a person could acquire self-respect simply by lowering her personal standards. But if self-respect depends on success according to standards which the person finds valuable, then it is implausible to allow that self-respect can be generated by a lowering of standards. We do not choose what we value, and so it is implausible to claim that we can lower our standards so as to generate self-respect and still find these standards valuable.[6] While I agree that what we find valuable may not always appear to us to be malleable, that does not entail that it is not malleable. People can and do change their values over the course of their lives. Whether it is appropriate that they change their values and generate self-respect by lowering their individual criteria of excellence is a question I do not answer here. All I want to allow for is that we might sometimes think that a person's lowering of her standards in pursuit of her self-respect makes sense and is appropriate. There is nothing prescriptive in allowing for this as a possibility.

Although congruence between a person's self-conception and her self-expression is an important and intuitively appealing aspect of self-respect, an account of self-respect just in terms of congruence is inadequate. Self-respect is also importantly connected with the *status* that a person takes herself to have. The inadequacy of characterising self-respect just in terms of congruence can be seen by considering the puzzle laid out in the next section.

3.3 Self-respect and the Stepford Wives

I shall consider a puzzle about self-respect which arises when it is characterised just in terms of congruence by comparing two examples. First, consider Harriet Taylor, long-term partner and eventual wife of John Stuart Mill. Most scholars agree that Taylor and Mill co-authored important pieces on women's rights, and marriage and divorce law.[7] Although her marriage to Mill was successful, Harriet Taylor was not happy in her first marriage, and was unable to marry Mill until after the death of her first husband, some twenty years after she and Mill first met. She was not a heroic figure and she was for most of her life stuck in a marriage from which she could not escape. Furthermore, she lived in Victorian society suffused with stifling norms governing what women could do. However, her involvement with Mill suggests that she had a conception of herself that was not wholly dictated to by these norms, and, let us suppose, she acted in congruence with this conception in a way supportive of her self-respect: she maintained a friendship with Mill which eventually led to marriage, and she expressed her views about equality for women in writing. The question of whether these details are historically accurate is not apposite here: let us assume that Harriet Taylor had self-respect through congruence, for the reasons I have just laid out.

Second, consider the Stepford Wives.[8] Ignoring the fact that the Stepford Wives in the film were automata, these are women who perform well at all the activities at the heart of their self-conceptions: they are maestros at washing up, masters of cake baking and geniuses at keeping their husbands fed, clothed and sexually satisfied. As one of the Stepford husbands in the film says of his Wife, 'She cooks as good as she looks'. The Stepford Wives are not unhappy; to the contrary, they take pleasure in devoting themselves to the well-being and success of their husbands, and take pride in the fact of this devotion.

Considering these descriptions just in the light of a congruence-based conception of self-respect, it should follow that Harriet Taylor and the Stepford Wives respect themselves to more or less the same degree, because they all achieve congruence between their self-conceptions and their self-expressions: Taylor managed to express, and live according to, her convictions about equality for women, and no one touches the Stepford Wives when it comes to house and husband keeping. But do we really want to make this unqualified claim? A conception of self-respect just in terms of congruence demands it, and yet there is something disturbing about treating the Stepford Wives as paradigm self-respecters. If our worries about the Stepford Wives are well grounded then there must be something true of Taylor which is not true of the Stepford Wives which explains this unease. Pinpointing this something will pave the way for a more substantive and fine-grained understanding of the intuitive thought about self-respect.

At first sight there are four ways to explain the difference between Taylor and the Stepford Wives. First, we could focus on what they *do*. Second, we could concentrate on the extent to which they *exercise certain capacities*. Third, we could address the *nature of their preferences*. And fourth, we could examine how they *feel*. I shall argue that each of these approaches has counter-intuitive implications, and that the best explanation of the difference between Taylor and the Stepford Wives reveals the sense in which a person's sense of her own status is necessary for her self-respect.[9]

The most obvious way to explain the difference between Taylor and the Stepford Wives is simply to claim that activities promoting equality for women in the face of Victorian prejudice are more worthy of respect than housekeeping, and that this claim is true regardless of the value that anyone takes housekeeping and Victorian feminism to have. On this account, Taylor respects herself more than the Stepford Wives because her attitude of respect towards herself *qua* Victorian feminist is more well-grounded than their attitudes of respect towards themselves *qua* housewives.

This is an undesirable approach to the problem. Why should *self*-respect depend upon the mind-independent value that different personal achievements have? Even if housekeeping really is value-inferior to challenging prejudiced dogma (or vice versa), this does not explain why we think that a group of housekeepers respect *themselves* less than a Victorian feminist (or vice versa). I believe it is better – really, truly better – for a person to devote her life to music than to God, but I do not therefore conclude that all success-ful pianists respect themselves more than a community of chaste Carmelites. Furthermore, the claim that self-respect depends on the mind-independent value of activities providing a putative basis for self-respect makes it possible to universally divorce persons' aware-ness of their self-respect from their possession of it. The claim that something has mind-independent value entails that it has value regardless and independent of the value any person takes it to have. This makes it possible for all self-respecting people to be unaware that they have self-respect, because they do not value the genuinely valuable activities upon which their self-respect is based.

Biting the bullet, it could be claimed that this is indeed a real possibility with respect to self-respect. But this seems implausible. Self-respect is a self-regarding state; to claim that a person could be in this state without having any awareness of it – indeed, could be in this state and deny it outright – seems odd. The objection is not that self-regarding states *per se* should not be characterised in this way: to the contrary, it is often the case that people are in a state of self-deception without any awareness of this fact. Rather, the reason why anyone should care about their self-respect seems connected with the idea that a self-respecting person is in some way aware of the fact that she has self-respect, and that she somehow draws strength from this awareness. The sense in which self-respect must be epistemically available to people will emerge in the discussion of self-respect and practical reason in the next chapter, where I argue that reflection on the self-conception at the heart of self-respect provides the context for practical reasoning about questions of justice.

The defender of this first strategy for solving the puzzle of the Stepford Wives could protest that what she meant by claiming that certain activities provide truly better grounds for self-respect than others is that some activities are more suited than others for encouraging the development and exercise of certain capacities, and the exercise of these capacities has mind-independent value. The claim now is that the difference between Taylor and the Stepford Wives is that Taylor has, or exercises, certain capacities that the Stepford Wives lack or fail to exercise; for example, the capacity to think for oneself. In virtue of how it connects self-respect with mind-independent value, this strategy is open to the same objection levelled against the last one. But putting this to one side, we might learn more about self-respect by considering what sorts of capacities might be claimed to ground it.

One obvious candidate is the capacity for autonomy, understood as self-determination independent of social standards.[10] The Stepford Wives live their lives according to social norms which prioritise the interests of their husbands, whereas (the argument would go) Taylor stands alone and thinks for herself. Thus Taylor has more self-respect than the Stepford Wives. The main problem with this account is that we can generate counter-intuitive cases of people who are independent of social norms and self-determining, but of whom it would seem peculiar to say that they have self-respect: the committed anorexic, the mistress who lives for her lover to leave his wife when he never will, or the fast-living, drug taking wild child who offers herself sexually to all comers. But it might also be the case that the Stepford Wives have autonomously chosen a life of devotion to their husbands independent of norms of female emancipation, which they have considered and rejected, in which case they exhibit autonomy-as-independence. The extent to which a life is led according to, or in contravention of, social norms does not in itself seem relevant to the question of whether that life is self-respecting.

The third approach claims that a person cannot have self-respect unless the preferences she acts upon in pursuing valued goals are authentic. One prominent account of authentic preferences defines them as objectively contributing to the development of the person according to a teleological conception;[11] for example, a Millean conception of the person as flourishing when she develops herself as a creative and independent being through the exercise of her freedom. It could be argued, then, that Taylor's preferences for Victorian feminism contribute to her flourishing as an individual whereas the Stepford Wives' preferences for catering for their husbands to the exclusion of all else do not, and thus Taylor has, and the Stepford Wives lack, self-respect.

One clear problem with this approach is the oddness of construing Taylor's commitment to female emancipation, and the Stepford Wives' commitment to caring for their husbands, just in terms of a set of preferences, however authentic. The language of preference seems too superficial to capture the nature of such commitments. However, allowing that this may be dismissed as a merely terminological worry, we can still criticise the authenticity based approach on grounds similar to those on which we criticised the other two approaches. The authenticity based approach requires a description of self-respect in terms of one very specific – in this case Millean-liberal – set of values. The claim must be that only those who satisfy preferences oriented towards Millean flourishing are candidate self-respecters. But (1) this allows self-respect to be entirely divorced from a person's awareness of it, and more importantly, (2) it is inadequate as an account fit to fill the motivational gap in the many flowers interpretation of the last chapter. If self-respect depends on flourishing in a Millean sense then accepting pluralism as a permanent fact in virtue of the acknowledgement that people care about their self-respect will give toleration and public reason a very limited scope. If self-respect is understood in this way then people only have reason to tolerate Millean conceptions of the good, and only have reason to endorse public reason with others who share the Millean view of flourishing. The many flowers view requires a more permissive account of what is wrong with the Stepford Wives. Is there such an account?

One possibility is to take an entirely different tack and claim that Taylor and the Stepford Wives differ only in how well they think of themselves and their achievements in relation to others. On this approach, Taylor would be understood as self-respecting in virtue of the fact that she thinks of herself as better than other women in her repressed Victorian society. The Wives, on the other hand, are meek and compliant, suggesting that they think of themselves as insignificant and of little consequence in comparison with other women. This account of self-respect might be supplemented with claims about the phenomenology of self-respecters. For example, it might be claimed that self-respect is accompanied by feelings of self-satisfaction or contentment.

The analysis of self-respect given by this account conflates self-respect and self-esteem.[12] The foundations of the currently fashionable concept of self-esteem are best understood in the psychologist William James' terms. James claimed that self-esteem depends on the ratio of a person's successes to her aspirations, such that the more successful a person is at achieving her goals, the greater the esteem in which she will hold herself.[13] There are two things wrong with this approach. First, it cannot explain our unease about the Stepford Wives for – it was stipulated – the Wives are extremely successful at housekeeping, just as successful – we could claim – as Taylor is in living according to her feminist values, given her circumstances. So focusing on the degree to which the Wives' deeds fulfil their aspirations cannot distinguish them from Taylor. If the analysis of self-respect as self-esteem is accompanied by an account of the phenomenology of self-respect so understood, then the account becomes even less plausible: neither Taylor nor the Stepford Wives need be thought of as feeling discontented.

To see the second problem with this approach we have to note that it places no constraints on the nature of the goals achievement of which contributes to self-esteem. This means that the achievement of any goal forming part of an aspiration is a candidate contributor to self-respect; any goal can be supportive of self-respect. But does a person's success in achieving her slavish goals support her self-respect? Success in achieving her sado-masochistic goals? Or goals involving self-destruction? It may contingently be the case that all those who respect themselves also hold themselves in esteem; we may also be able to make a moral argument that self-respect always provides a ground for self-esteem. But the reverse of these claims are not obviously true, as we can see by reconsidering our reactions to the Stepford Wives. We can admit that the Stepford Wives esteem themselves and still have worries over their self-respect. The possibility – indeed, likelihood – of a constant conjunction of self-respect and self-esteem has no implications for the identity of the concepts.[14]

So exactly what is wrong with the Stepford Wives? What is it that they have or do which would explain our reluctance to point them out to children as self-respecting role models? One plausible explanation of the Wives' overwhelming desires to promote their husbands' interests is that the Wives conceive of their husbands as more valuable than them, or that they think of themselves as inferior in status to their husbands. In other words, the Wives are subservient.[15] The same is not true of Harriet Taylor. By locating the self-respect related difference between the Stepford Wives and Harriet Taylor in their sense of status we can explain why our judgements with respect to their self-respect differ while avoiding the problems raised by the explanations considered earlier. (Of course, our judgement of the two cases could be wrong. Perhaps the Wives behave as they do out of a concern for the well-being of their children, or perhaps they simply adore their husbands; and perhaps Taylor lived her life for Mill in a slavish and self-destructive way. My aim here is not to make a definitive judgement of these two cases, but rather to explain why we judge differently in each case, given the assumption that we do.)

This explanation also works with respect to other problem cases. For example, if we think that an anorexic who achieves congruence nevertheless lacks self-respect, why do we pause before making the same judgement of the IRA hunger-striker Bobby Sands?[16] Both people achieve congruence through refusing to eat, and, for the reasons given above, an account of *self*-respect should not be tied to an account of the comparative worth of different ways of life. A more plausible explanation of the difference in our judgements is that anorexics typically have a damaged sense of their status relative to others, as evinced in the self-loathing and depression which often accompanies this condition. But Bobby Sands' self-destruction was a form of political protest reflecting the strength of his political convictions: Bobby Sands did not starve himself to death because he hated himself, but because he was opposed to what he saw as the illegitimacy of British rule in Northern Ireland. Or consider self-harmers – those who cut their arms, for example – who achieve congruence in comparison with performance artists who engage in similar activities. Again, the best explanation of why we would judge each case differently lies in our different judgements of the sense of their own status that each sort of person typically has.

So, making a sense of status central to the account of self-respect has initial plausibility. But we need to flesh out in more detail what is involved in this sense of status, and how we tell whether a person has it or lacks it. I propose the following interpretation.

> A person conceives of herself as having less status than others when she would judge as illegitimate any expectation of hers that others offer her justifying reasons why she should perform actions which she is expected by them to perform.

Given this understanding, the problem with the self-respect of the Stepford Wives is that they would think that it is illegitimate for a Wife to expect that her husband should offer her justifying reasons why she should make the sacrifices she does in caring for him. We can put the claim positively: a person conceives of herself as having similar status to others when she would judge as legitimate any expectation of hers that others should offer her justifying reasons why she should perform actions which she is expected by them to perform, were she to have such an expectation. This characterisation of non-subservience is supposed to capture the idea that a person with a sense of her own status has a sense of herself as worthy of being given reasons. Let me pause here for a few reflections on this way of understanding subservience and non-subservience in relation to self-respect.

First, it is important to clarify the sense in which the reasons referred to in this account are justifying. There are two ways we might understand this.[17]

(1) A reason might be justifying in a person-relative sense. Here, the fact that a person takes a reason to be justifying is sufficient for it to be justifying. The problem is that this warrants counter-intuitive judgements in cases which are taken to be paradigms of subservience, such as the Stepford Wives. Here, the drudge wife may well take her dominant husband's 'Because I say so' to be a justifying reason for whatever he asks of her, and therefore count as non-subservient. So it is better to understand the justifying reasons of this account of subservience in a non person-relative way.

(2) When a reason is justifying in a non person-relative way then it is not sufficient for that reason to be justifying that a person takes it to be justifying. This prevents the counter-intuitive judgements entailed by (1), but it raises the question of which reasons count as justifying. What is needed is an account of justifying reasons as non-person relative which also rules out as justifying the sorts of reasons that subservient people are often offered in a sham of an exchange of reasons. For example, a Stepford Husband may say to his Wife, 'You must cook dinner for my boss and his wife tomorrow because I say so'; or, 'You must leave your career because you are my wife now'; or, 'You must perform this sexual act because I want you to.' We have established that the question of whether a Wife would take such reasons to be justifying is not relevant to the question of whether they are justifying. So, are such reasons justifying?

There are various accounts of justifying reasons in the literature according to which such reasons are not justifying. I do not propose to trawl through them here, because what matters from my point of view is that there is no philosophical account of justifying reasons which endorses the ones just given as justifying *tout court*, and this is because an such account would clash with our moral experience. To see why, consider the following examples.

We might think that 'because I say so' is genuinely justifying when offered by a parent to a child, by a commanding officer to an unruly cadet, or by a quick-thinking heroine in a disaster situation when there is no time for discussion, and her companions' lives are on the line. These examples of circumstances in which we think 'because I say so' would serve as a justifying reason tell us something about the circumstances in which we think it would not serve. In the example of the parent and child, the child is not capable of properly judging whether what the parent asks is in her interests or not, whereas the parent is in such a position. And so we think the parent's indication to the child that she has a reason to do what the parent asks just because it is the parent who is doing the asking is a justifying reason. But note here that we think that this relationship between parent and child is temporary: at some point, we think that a parent should do more than respond to her child's request for reasons with a 'because I say so'. In the case of the commanding officer and the unruly cadet, we think that the CO offers a justifying reason when he says 'because I say so' because it is part of what it is to be a CO that such reasons are genuinely justifying when offered to junior staff: without the possibility of senior staff giving orders, military organisation would collapse. But note that we would not think it to be appropriate that 'because I say so' is a justifying reason for the junior cadet in all circumstances, and we expect the junior cadet to understand this. For example, we do not think that the cadet is blameless if he steals or rapes under order: we do not think that 'I was just obeying orders' absolves military personnel of personal responsibility for what they do in all circumstances. In the case of the disaster situation we might think that 'because I say so' serves as a justifying reason when the person who offers it to her fellows has information crucial to their survival that they lack, or can see the looming danger that they cannot. But note that we think of such circumstances as exceptional ones in which the importance of survival combined with the need for leadership and speedy action make deliberation between the parties inappropriate. In non-disaster situations, where time is not of the essence and joint decisions have to be made, we do not think that 'because I say so' is a justifying reason given by a quick-thinking heroine; rather, we would think of such a person as arrogant and bossy.

These examples suggest that any account of justifying reasons which endorses 'because I say so' – and cognate reasons which are offered as reasons just in virtue of who it is who is doing the offering – as genuinely justifying for persons not in special circumstances or relationships like those outlined above will not fit our moral experience. And, in fact, I can think of no such account in the literature. If there is no such account then building the non-subservience component into the account of self-respect makes self-respect, thus far at least, a value which is compatible with various different substantive accounts of justifying reasons. If all of these accounts have it in common that, *ceteris paribus*, justifying reasons cannot count as justifying just in virtue of who it is who offers them as justifying, then there is no need to specify in any more detail what it takes for a reason to be justifying, because on any account of this, the reasons that subservient people settle for *qua* subservient are not justifying.

The second important thing to note is that my account of subservience should not be taken to suggest that non-subservient people are constantly demanding reasons from those who have expectations of them. Non-subservient people should not be conceived of as shrill harpies who make other people's lives unbearable with unending demands for reasons. The counterfactuality of the claim means that a person can be non-subservient without actually having expectations that others provide her with these reasons: what matters instead is how she would judge these expectations were she to have them. Of course, most non-subservient people will sometimes have these expectations, and voice them. But to stipulate that the non-subservient person must actually have expectations that she be given reasons which she judges legitimate is too demanding: the character or external circumstances of some people may simply never prompt these expectations.[18] But we should not conclude from this that they are subservient.

Third, it might be thought that this way of understanding non-subservience makes anyone who has ever been in love, or loved a child, subservient. Surely the lover would not think it legitimate for her to ask her loved one why she should do what he expects her to do? I think that a person experiencing a love which prevents them from making the judgement that a request for reasons would be legitimate is in danger of being used, as subservient people tend to be used. Love can be true without the lovers being subservient to one another. As we have seen, the fact that a lover would judge her request for reasons to be legitimate does not mean that she will actually demand these reasons and, furthermore, it does not mean that she will subject them to hard-nosed scrutiny if she receives them, as if making spelling corrections to a love letter. Love can, of course, lead people to subjugate themselves to one another, but – as we know from countless novels, poems, and films – such love can also be destructive and damaging to the lovers.

With respect to children, it is clear that young children do not have the capacity to provide others with reasons why they should perform certain actions. But children at this stage of development cannot be said to have 'expectations' of others at all: it would be perverse of a parent to judge as legitimate her expectation that her child provide her with reasons indexed to its non-existent expectations. However, at some stage children do develop expectations and the concomitant capacity to give reasons which support these expectations. At this point I think we would expect parents to judge as legitimate their own expectations that their children provide them with appropriate reasons. (In fact, given the unpleasantness of a spoiled and indulged child, we would want parents to *actually* ask their children to provide these reasons. However, this is not strictly necessary for parental non-subservience.) Without non-subservience, parents can become drudges to their children just as much as the lover can become a doormat for the loved one.

Finally, note that my analysis does not interpret subservience in terms of a comprehensive doctrine stating the nature of human equality. This means that the value of non-subservience is not the prerogative of any particular religious believers, moral converts, or philosophical disciples. If it is possible for a person to ask for a reason, then it is possible for that person to be subservient or non-subservient, and the capacity to ask for reasons is not peculiar to the conception of the person associated with any particular set of moral, philosophical, or religious beliefs.

Self-respect requires congruence and a sense of status: in conjunction, these conditions are sufficient for self-respect. Each of these aspects of self-respect is connected with practical reasoning as it addresses questions of justice. An account of this connection and its significance will be given in the next chapter. For now, let me highlight how the congruence aspect of self-respect informs Rawls' account of the social bases of self-respect, as the most developed account in the literature.

3.4   Rawlsian self-respect

Rawls' conception of self-respect is an elaboration of the congruence component of self-respect, and is worth examining just on this account. However, my primary interest in Rawls' account is with respect to his remarks on the social contexts in which self-respect is developed. It is here, I think, that Rawls has real insights. Adapting some of his remarks on these social contexts will support – in the next chapter – an explanation of why those who accept the permanence of pluralism in virtue of accepting the diverse ways in which self-respect can be developed and maintained could not reject reasons to practice toleration and to endorse public reason. Clarifying the dynamics of these social contexts provides the linchpin of this argument.

Rawls claims that self-respect is 'perhaps the most important primary good'[19] and that:

> [Self-respect] first of all…includes a person's sense of his own value, his secure conviction that his conception of the good, his plan of life, is worth carrying out. And second, self-respect implies a confidence in one's ability, so far as it is within one's power, to fulfil one's intentions. When we feel that our plans are of little value, we cannot pursue them with pleasure or take delight in their execution. Nor plagued by failure and self-doubt can we continue in our endeavours.[20]

With respect to congruence, Rawls claims that self-respect depends upon:

> (1) Having a rational plan of life, and in particular one that satisfies the Aristotelian principle; and (2) finding our own person and deeds appreciated and confirmed by others who are likewise esteemed and their association enjoyed.[21]

There are three aspects of Rawls' characterisation of the success related to self-respect that require clarification: the sense of 'rationality', the nature of the Aristotelian principle, and the role of what I shall call 'the conditions of reciprocal esteem'.

The fully rational plan of life for any individual is, says Rawls:

> the one that would be chosen [by the agent] with full deliberative rationality, that is, with full awareness of the relevant facts and after careful consideration of the consequences.[22]

'Full deliberative rationality' refers to the choice of life plans in hypothetical conditions wherein all the facts relevant to that life plan are available to the chooser and the chooser takes the most effective means to the ends she adopts in the light of this knowledge. Full deliberative rationality is not what grounds self-respect in Rawls' account. A person may suffer regret if she pursues a plan to which she eventually discovers she is not suited, but the fact that she failed to spot in advance that her plan was unsuitable for her need not detract from her self-respect. The rationality that matters for Rawlsian self-respect is subjective and reflects our epistemological limitations. As Rawls says, 'if the agent does the best that a rational person can do with the information available to him, then the plan he follows is a subjectively rational plan'.[23]

Subjective rationality matters for Rawlsian self-respect because of its connection with the Aristotelian principle. The Aristotelian principle tells us what kinds of ends constitute rational plans of life by stating a principle of human motivation. To that extent it also helps to explain common and important human desires. The principle is that:

> other things being equal, human beings enjoy the exercise of their realized capacities (their innate or trained abilities), and this enjoyment increases the more the capacity is realized, or the greater its complexity.[24]

An example of someone meeting the Aristotelian principle, thinks Rawls, is a person able to play both chess and draughts but who prefers to play chess because of the superior demands it makes on him and his abilities. Anyone satisfying the Aristotelian principle has developed, will develop, or will continue to develop and refine the talents and assets which promote ends forming part of their rational plan of life.

Satisfying the Aristotelian principle matters for self-respect because such satisfaction is likely to prompt the respect of others, and, Rawls thinks, receiving the respect of others is conducive to self-respect.[25] The fact that others believe that a person is of worth and have confidence in her abilities to pursue the plans which they themselves want to pursue encourages the development of the person's self-respect. As Rawls puts it:

> the conditions for persons respecting themselves and one another would seem to require that their common plans be rational and

complementary: they call upon their educated endowments and arouse in each a sense of mastery, and they fit together into one scheme of activity that all can appreciate and enjoy.[26]

The conditions of reciprocal esteem are self-replicating. A person whose self-respect is supported by the esteem and admiration of others will, to put it crudely, be more likely to return the compliment than if she lacked such self-respect, and this disposition on her part will indirectly work to her benefit by disposing others, in virtue of their self-respect, to be more forthcoming with their praise. 'One who is confident in himself is not grudging in the appreciation of others'.[27]

That Rawls connects self-respect to the development of refined and intricate talents and achievement in communities of shared interests does not make self-respect the prerogative of artistic, scientific or commercial high-fliers. As Rawls says, 'the application of the Aristotelian principle is always relative to the individual and therefore to his natural assets and particular situation'.[28] The conditions of reciprocal esteem can therefore be generated by communities of shared interests who would perhaps be judged poorly in competition with other communities of shared interests organised around similar pursuits. What counts as an excellence fit to elicit the esteem of others will all depend on who you ask.[29]

Another important feature of the Aristotelian principle is that when the search for self-respect is successful, a person's self-conception is reaffirmed, but not in a way that suggests that self-respecters smugly sit on their laurels and never develop their talents further. The dynamism of individual criteria of excellence which satisfy the Aristotelian principle explains how the sources of self-respect in a person's self-conception evolve and change over time. Success according to one set of criteria leads to changes in the requirements or complexity of the criteria which can accumulate so as to eventually constitute a new and very different self-conception as the basis of a person's self-respect.

These two features reflect the fact that Rawls' account of self-respect is congruence based. Rawls' stipulations that self-respect requires success according to a subjectively rational life plan governed by the Aristotelian principle do not provide him with a way of distinguishing between the Stepford Wives and Harriet Taylor. The house and husband keeping activities of the Wives can be developed and honed in line with the Aristotelian principle just as well as the feminist activities of Harriet Taylor. For Rawls, self-respect involves a person being confident in her abilities to carry out her life plans, and involves a sense that these plans are worth carrying out. People normally engage in these activities in communities of shared interests, where they judge themselves more or less successful at these activities according to standards relativised to the abilities of members of these communities. A person's self-respect is supported by membership of such communities when she succeeds in activities around which the group is organised, and which, given her membership of the group, inform her self-conception.

Although Rawls conceives of those who seek self-respect supporting congruence as members of communities of shared interests, it does not follow that he conceives of the success that matters for self-respect as success according to social standards of excellence à la Nozick. There is no suggestion on Rawls' part that we *must* stake our self-respect on success according to the standards implicit in any or each of the communities of shared interests in which we participate. Instead, our self-respect depends on 'finding our own person and deeds appreciated and confirmed by others who are likewise esteemed and their association enjoyed'.[30] That is, our self-respect depends on success according to the standards adopted by those with whom we identify ourselves. If we do not identify ourselves with many of the communities in which we participate then failure according to the standards of these communities will be irrelevant for self-respect. If we do not identify ourselves with *any* communities then our self-respect affecting standards will have no social aspect at all. Of course there are, in reality, very few genuine hermits, and of those that there are it is reasonable to think that there are very few self-respecters. Shunning the world is more indicative of a person's lack of confidence and sense of her own status than the reverse. Alternatively, there are very few people who, as a result of their own effort, are undoubted and esteemed successes in their communities (and who know this) who would claim to lack self-respect. Nonetheless, both cases provide a possible framework for self-respect.[31]

Rawls' account of the congruence aspect of self-respect and its social contexts is psychologically plausible. So long as we remember that congruence must be achieved against the background of a non-subservient self-conception (which will prove to be important in the next chapter), the details of Rawls' account can be used to fill the motivational gap in the many flowers interpretation. Before turning to that in the next chapter, let me briefly outline how Rawls uses the idea of self-respect and its social bases in the political justification of *A Theory of Justice* and *Political Liberalism*. (I shall give a more detailed account of the social bases of self-respect in Chapter 5.)

In both *A Theory of Justice* and *Political Liberalism* Rawls claims that principles of justice distribute social primary goods.[32] In *A Theory of Justice* these goods are characterised as 'things that every rational man is presumed to want';[33] in *Political Liberalism*, as 'essential all-purpose means to realize the higher-order interests connected with citizens' moral powers and their determinate conceptions of the good'.[34] In both cases, primary goods provide people with the means for the pursuit of their conception of the good, whatever it is. Thus, primary goods can be used to make interpersonal comparisons of advantage for the purposes of assessing whether a given distribution of goods is just or unjust. Rawls' list of primary goods is: basic rights and liberties, freedom of movement and free choice of occupation, income and wealth, and the social bases of self-respect. Principles of justice distribute these goods. With respect to self-respect, Rawls claims that:

> self-respect depends upon and is encouraged by certain public features of basic social institutions, how they work together and how people who accept these arrangements are expected to (and normally do) regard and treat one another. These features of basic institutions and publicly expected (and normally honoured) ways of conduct are the social bases of self-respect.[35]

Rawls claims that the social bases of self-respect are 'perhaps the most important primary good',[36] are of 'fundamental importance',[37] and are 'among the most essential [of the] primary goods'.[38,39] The social bases of self-respect are of this importance because of the importance of self-respect *per se*: I shall offer an account of this importance which is consistent with the many flowers view in the next chapter. For now, let me sketch how Rawls understands the social bases of self-respect and their role in his political justification.

The social bases of self-respect are distributed by the principles of justice, which shape the basic structure of society. Rawls' two principles of justice are:

a. Each person has an equal right to a fully adequate scheme of equal basic liberties which is compatible with a similar scheme of liberties for all.
b. Social and economic inequalities are to satisfy two conditions. First, they must be attached to offices and positions open to all under conditions of fair equality of opportunity; and second, they must be to the greatest benefit of the least advantaged members of society.[40]

The first principle distributes basic rights and liberties (including freedom of movement) and the second principle distributes free choice of occupation, and income and wealth. There is no principle of justice which directly addresses the distribution of the social bases of self-respect. Instead, Rawls thinks that the distribution of primary goods specified by his principles of justice provides the supervenience base for the distribution of the social bases of self-respect. In other words, any difference between people in terms of their access to the social bases of self-respect is to be explained by differences between them in terms of their basic rights and liberties, their freedom of movement and free choice of occupation, and their income and wealth.

This supervenience claim can be made clearer with a typology of the social bases of self-respect. Rawls claims that:

> The account of self-respect as perhaps the most important primary good has stressed the great significance of how we think others value us. But in a well-ordered society the need for status is met by the public recognition of just institutions, together with the full and diverse internal life of the many free communities of interests that equal liberty allows.[41]

Joshua Cohen suggests that the social bases of self-respect be understood as follows.[42] 'Resource' bases of self-respect are practical means which enable people to develop themselves according to their non-subservient self-conceptions. 'Recognitional' bases of self-respect are the attitudes of others towards the person that support and foster her non-subservient self-conception. Both resource and recognitional bases of self-respect can be found either in the associational or in the framework conditions of society. The associational bases of self-respect are the communities of shared interests providing the conditions of reciprocal esteem, and the framework bases are 'the framework of institutions and associated forms of public argument [which] support and foster the associational conditions'.[43]

This classification helps us to understand when stage 1 principles secure the social bases of self-respect. Principles are to be assessed (1) according to how they promote the resource and recognitional bases of self-respect in aspects of the basic structure, and (2) according to how they promote these bases within communities of shared interests. Given that the basic structure is the subject of justice for Rawls, the associational bases of self-respect in (2) can only be provided through aspects of the basic structure; it is the effect that principles have on the basic structure alone that determines whether they secure the social bases of self-respect. The question is whether the basic structure of society under *this* conception of justice will itself provide people with opportunity for self-respect, and whether it will also encourage the formation and development of communities of shared interests outside of the basic structure to provide them with associational bases of self-respect.

A further clarification. Rawls claims that the social bases of self-respect are included on the list of primary goods subject to *maximin* distribution. This means that inequalities in the social bases of self-respect are allowed only if these inequalities work to the advantage of the worst off group in terms of their social bases of self-respect. But note that this does not entail either of the following claims. First, that some inequalities in the distribution of some primary goods on which social bases of self-respect supervene necessarily create a non-maximin distribution of the social bases of self-respect. And second, that a strictly equal distribution of all primary goods upon which the social bases of self-respect supervene guarantees a maximin distribution of the social bases of self-respect. In other words, a maximin distribution of the social bases of self-respect need not require that each of the goods in the supervenience base for the social bases of self-respect be given an equal distribution. To assess whether a maximin strategy with respect to the social bases of self-respect demands an equal distribution of *all* goods constitutive of these social bases requires a clarification of the way in which *each* of these goods provide opportunities for self-respect. The distribution of the goods of basic rights and liberties, and income and wealth, will be discussed as supervenience bases for a maximin distribution of the social bases of self-respect in Chapter 5.

With an account of self-respect and its social bases in hand we are now in a position to give an account of the importance of self-respect to people facing problems of justice together that is consistent with the many flowers view. To be consistent with this view, those who accept the importance of self-respect to themselves and to others cannot do so on the grounds that a self-respecting life promotes just one particular set of values or ideals. Acceptance of the permanence of pluralism on these grounds would limit the scope of the toleration and public reason that such people have reason to practice, given the importance they acknowledge that self-respect and its social conditions has for them and others. On the many flowers view, stage 2 people must accept the significance of self-respect on grounds that do not discriminate between different paths to self-respect by reference to any particular comprehensive theory of the good. At the very least, the importance which ideal people attach to self-respect must require less uniformity among them on key questions of philosophy and value than that demanded by the incommensurability and burdens views outlined at the end of the last chapter.

What I shall propose in the next chapter is that stage 2 people should be understood as acknowledging the significance that others' self-respect has for them because self-respect provides materials without which a person could not reason practically about problems of justice. Self-respect – in both its congruence and its non-subservience aspects – provides the context necessary for the peaceful resolution of problems of justice through the use of reason. Without self-respect, I shall argue, stage 2 people could not be thought of as engaging in the practice of political justification: self-respect is an idea of practical reason as it addresses problems of justice.

This account of the significance of self-respect does not discriminate between the different paths to self-respect: each congruent, non-subservient path can provide a person with grounds for self-respect. *Prima facie*, this creates a problem for the account because it seems to allow for paths to self-respect which also lead to intolerance and a rejection of public reason. This is a problem because the account was supposed to supply the motivational deficit in the many flowers view by explaining why commitment to self-respect means that a person could not reject reasons to practice tolerance and endorse public reason. It is here that the social contexts in which self-respect is developed become important: focusing on them fills the motivational gap.

4
Reasoning about Justice

4.1 Introduction

The arguments of this chapter will be that (1) self-respect is an idea of practical reason as it addresses problems of justice; (2) that the social contexts in which self-respect is developed mean that self-respecting people could not reject reasons to practice toleration and endorse public reason; and (3) that these features of self-respect mean that those who seek an explanation of why ideal people accept the permanence of pluralism that is less demanding than the incommensurability or burdens view should make the self-respect of ideal people a prominent feature of stage 2 of the Constructivist procedure of justification. If (1)–(3) can be established then the account of a minimally demanding liberal Constructivism sketched in Chapter 2 will have been delivered. Let me spell this out in a little more detail.

This chapter and the previous one build up to the argument at the end of this chapter that conceiving of persons as self-respecters for the purposes of political justification is less demanding than conceiving of them as accepting incommensurability or the burdens of judgement. In this chapter I shall argue that a person's self-respect provides the context necessary for practical reasoning about matters of justice; that is, that we cannot conceive of persons as exercising their practical reason when facing problems of justice unless we conceive of them as having and caring about their self-respect (sections 4.2–4.3). This establishes that Constructivist approaches to political justification must include a commitment to self-respect as an aspect of stage 2 persons. Then I shall argue that self-respecting people could not reject reasons to practice toleration and endorse public reason in virtue of the social dynamics of self-respect. This establishes that a Constructivism which includes a commitment to self-respect as an aspect of stage 2 persons can deliver liberal results. Finally, I shall argue that a liberal Constructivism which makes self-respect central to the stage 2 conception of the person can explain why ideal people accept the permanence of pluralism in a less demanding way than a Constructivism reliant on the incommensurability or burdens views of the permanence of pluralism. In Chapter 1 I stipulated that political justification ought to be addressed to a deeply diverse constituency. If the many flowers view which emphasises self-respect is less demanding than the burdens or incommensurability views, then it is to be preferred on the grounds that it allows for more diversity in the constituency of justification than the alternative views, and is just as successful as they are in justifying liberal principles (section 4.5).

Let me start by outlining how self-respect provides a context for practical reasoning about problems of justice. This account means that there is a good reason for including commitment to self-respect as an aspect of the stage 2 person, regardless of the level of demandingness of the many flowers view to which, I shall argue, it is central. On this account, stage 2 persons who face unavoidable problems of justice together, which must be solved through the exercise of practical reason, must be assumed to have and to care about their self-respect. Let me start by suggesting where a person's self-respect might have a role to play in her practical reasoning *per se* (section 4.2) before going on to explore the connection between self-respect and justice-oriented practical reasoning (section 4.3).

4.2   Self-respect and practical reason

Practical reason is the capacity to set ends and deliberate about means to these ends. When a person sets herself an end, rather than just discovering herself with this end, she endorses reasons for the pursuit of that end according to which she takes the end to be appropriate for her. Similarly, when a person reasons practically about the best means to her ends, she considers the extent to and way in which the various means over which she is deliberating will further her ends, and she endorses reasons for the adoption of the set of means which she takes to be the most effective with respect to the realisation of her ends. My strategy to show that self-respect provides the context for practical reasoning about problems of justice is (1) to break self-respect down into its two components – non-subservience and congruence – and consider in turn how they provide the context for what I shall call 'strongly evaluative' practical reasoning about problems of justice, and then (2) argue that practical reasoning about problems of justice is strongly evaluative.

Non-subservience and practical reason

To see the form of practical reasoning for which non-subservience provides a context, let us return to the subservient Stepford Wives. In the last chapter I gave the following account of subservience. The subservient person would judge as illegitimate any expectation of hers that others offer her justifying reasons why she should perform actions which she is expected by them to perform. Put positively: a non-subservient person would judge as legitimate any expectation of hers that others should offer her justifying reasons why she should perform actions which she is expected by them to perform.

What form of practical reasoning does subservience prevent? The subservient person would judge any expectation of hers that others give her justifying reasons to be illegitimate: this is why subservient people are doormats and drudges to others. A subservient person, then, is not in a position to ask others for reasons when they make practical demands or requests of her. This reveals the sense in which subservience interferes with practical reasoning as it addresses problems of justice. The practice of political justification requires an *exchange* of reasons between members of the constituency of justification. It requires that each person be in a position to ask those who propose principles which require action of her for justifying reasons which support these principles, and then that each person be in a position to assess these reasons once they are offered. The assessment of reasons in political justification is complex and will be addressed in the remainder of this section and the next. But the damage that subservience does to a person's capacity to reason practically about problems of justice is clear: subservience prevents a person from asking all or some (depending on the extent of her subservience) members of the constituency of justification for justifying reasons. If a person is not in a position to ask for these reasons then she is not in a position to assess them.

The problem with the subservient person is that she will not judge to be legitimate her expectations that those to whom she is subservient provide her with reasons for the demands they make of her (if, indeed, she has any such expectations). As these demands will relate to proposed solutions to problems of justice, the subservient person is not in a position to exchange political justifications with those to whom she is subservient. In effect, a person's subservience excludes her from membership of any constituency of justification with those to whom she is subservient. Given that liberals aim for inclusive constituencies of justification, they ought to be committed to creating social and political conditions which discourage all subservience. This removes one impediment to the exercise of practical reason in the exchange of political justifications.[1]

Once a person is in a position to ask others for reasons, she is in a position to assess these reasons. I shall now explore how self-respect informs such assessment in general before turning to its role in practical reasoning about problems of justice in particular.

Congruence and practical reason

When a practical reasoner deliberates over the reasons supporting the various ends and means between which she must choose, she assesses ends and means by assessing the reasons which support the adoption of these ends and means. Ends and means supported by reasons which convince the person that these ends and means are appropriate for her are, all else being equal, the ends and means that she will adopt. Adapting Charles Taylor's account of the assessment of reasons characteristic of human agency, we can think of such assessments as varying in their qualitative aspects in the following three ways.[2]

(1) Quantitative assessment

A person can be thought of as assessing reasons by comparing them in terms of a single value or good. On this account, one reason will be endorsed as better than another if the course of action it supports creates more of this value, or a greater amount of this good. For example, the value according to which a person assesses competing reasons might be the maximisation of her sensual pleasure. Given this value, she may choose to stay in bed for another hour rather than getting up now in order to work up an appetite for a leisurely, wine-accompanied lunch, on the grounds that staying in bed requires less effort than getting up for lunch and, for her, maximising her sensual pleasure requires minimising effort and activity. On this account, practical reasoning is a form of calculation: practical reasons are assessed along one dimension of value, and then compared according to the quantity of value that action for them (is likely to) create along this dimension.

Quantitative calculation is a matter of comparing options along the same dimension of value. But the value in terms of which options are compared need not be particularly dear to the calculating person, in which case the options she evaluates may have little significance for her. Quantitative comparisons between options commensurable in terms of a trivial value are common in practical reasoning ('which will fill me up more at lunch, a bowl of soup or a sandwich?'), as are such comparisons as a means of damage limitation ('which of these films which I am being forced to see by my teenage niece will be the least tedious, *Scary Movie*, or *The Mummy Returns*?').

Beyond quantitative assessment, there are at least two further types of evaluation in practical reasoning. (1) When the reasons a person assesses relate to courses of action both of which cannot be chosen, and the values expressed by each set of reasons lack significance for the person, the assessment is *weakly evaluative*. (2) When the reasons a person assesses relate to courses of action both of which may, but need not be, practically incompatible, and the assessment has significance in virtue of how the value(s) informing it reflect the self-conception at the heart of the person's self-respect, the assessment is *strongly evaluative*. Let me consider these further forms of evaluation in turn.

(2) Weak evaluation

In some cases of practical evaluation a person does not compare reasons along a single dimension of value, but rather chooses between reasons supporting courses of action which are contingently incompatible, and which express values that the person does not reduce to a master-value. In these cases, a person acknowledges the values expressed by the competing reasons as values, but does not attempt to compare them in terms of a further value, as she would if she were assessing them quantitatively. Instead, she focuses on the value that would be realised by each course of action in its own terms, and chooses between the options understood as outcomes.

Weakly evaluative choice often will be driven just by what the person most desires: she accepts that both options are valuable, but she just wants to do A more than B. Expressions like, 'I just felt like it', or 'the mood took me', capture the character of weak evaluation. Or – for an indecisive person, or one forced to choose quickly, or under duress – problems of weak evaluation may be solved by strategies like tossing a coin, or getting someone else to choose for her. These features of weak evaluation make sense of Taylor's claim that the language of weak evaluation is inarticulate and lacks depth.[3] When we choose on the basis of weak evaluation we cannot say with any great colour or feeling why we choose as we do.

Weakly evaluative judgements are appropriate grounds for choosing between options both of which an agent values, both of which she cannot pursue, but neither of which are *evaluatively significant* for her. A choice or decision has evaluative significance for a person when action for the reasons she evaluates forms part of, or is excluded by, the self-conception at the heart of her self-respect. To say that weak evaluation relates to decisions lacking evaluative significance is thus to say that, although the person cares (although not necessarily deeply) about which reason she eventually endorses, she does not conceive of this assessment as part of her conception of herself as a certain sort of person. Weak evaluation is not related to self-respect.

Quantitative assessment and weak evaluation capture the character of deliberation over options in many everyday exercises of practical reason: we often make our decisions by calculating odds for possible options against the background of a given set of aims, or by just trying to get clear about what it is we most want to do, or 'feel like' doing.[4] Most of a person's day-to-day decisions do not require evaluative agonising or soul searching. However, there are certain sorts of decisions for which, we feel, quantitative calculation or weak evaluation are inappropriate. Consider the following cases: the choice between pursuing a successful career abroad or staying to care for ageing parents; deliberation over whether to tell a friend about her husband's marital infidelity; the question of whether to put one's child in a private school despite a personal commitment to equality. The practical reasoning required in these sorts of cases does not normally involve quantitative calculation or weak evaluation. The egalitarian who justifies her decision to place her child in a private school by saying 'I just felt like it' fails to appreciate the evaluative significance either of her child's future, or of her commitment to equality. The person whose stance towards her parents is just governed by, for example, calculations of what would maximise her career success fails to consider the nature of her relationship with her parents, and what leaving might mean for that relationship. In cases like these, we think that a very different form of practical evaluation is called for: this is what Taylor calls 'strong evaluation'.

(3) Strong evaluation

When a person evaluates strongly she assesses what action for the reasons under consideration would mean for her conception of herself as a certain sort of person, and for her hopes about the sort of person she might become. Given any person's self-respect supporting self-conception, motivations to act for certain reasons will be ruled out: a person whose self-respect is staked on her conception of herself as a risk-taker who lives for the thrill of the moment will be motivationally resistant to the idea of taking a routine job for the sake of a more secure future, all else being equal. Of course, all else is often not equal, and the self-respect of most people is staked on a multi-faceted self-conception. In this case, the risk-taking self-respecter's self-conception may also include a commitment to provide for a child in the future, or a determination not to be financially dependent on hard-pressed relatives, or the state; these aspects of the person's self-conception may override her love of risk-taking, and lead her to take the routine job after all. As self-respect supporting self-conceptions are always complex and many-faceted, the outcome of any person's strongly evaluative practical reasoning can be hard to predict, and sometimes hard to understand from the outside.

Unlike weak evaluation, reasons ruled out by strong evaluation are not excluded just in virtue of how they conflict with other reasons which are also valued. Rather, certain reasons are ruled out because action for them would destroy a person's self-respect. As Taylor puts it with respect to courageous action:

> If we examine my evaluative vision more closely, we shall see that I value courageous action as part of a mode of life; I aspire to be a certain kind of person. This would be compromised by my giving

in to [a] craven impulse. Here there is incompatibility. But this incompatibility is no longer contingent. It is not just a matter of circumstances which makes it impossible to give in to the impulse to flee and still cleave to a courageous, upright mode of life. Such a mode of life consists among other things in withstanding such craven impulses.[5]

When a person strongly evaluates she considers what it would mean for her self-respect were she to act for the reason under evaluation in a 'vocabulary of worth' which does not operate in weak evaluation. The strong evaluator is able to describe the reasons she rejects as those of a coward, a traitor, a liar, a hypocrite, or a fool because her self-respect is based upon her conception of herself as brave, loyal, honest, sincere, or dignified. She has, as Taylor puts it, 'a language of evaluative distinctions' which the weak evaluator lacks.[6] Furthermore, that the strong evaluator's vocabulary of worth is derived from the self-conception forming the basis of her self-respect gives it a texture and richness lacked by the quantitative calculator, who aims to maximise value along a single dimension. The strong evaluator does not necessarily aim to maximise anything: rather, she aims to act for reasons congruent with her self-respect supporting conception of herself as a certain sort of person, and thus safeguard her future self-respect.

Unlike weak evaluation and quantitative assessment, reasons which are strongly evaluated have evaluative significance for the person. Strong evaluation is not at the heart of practical reasoning about everyday matters, and may be only intermittently present in a person's practical reasoning. A person whose practical reasoning is a matter of constant or near-constant strong evaluation would resemble Kant's 'fantastically virtuous [person] who allows nothing to be morally indifferent and strews all his steps with duties, as with mantraps';[7] for such a person, all practical decisions would be a matter of self-respect. This would paralyse day-to-day decision-making, as well as probably driving any such deliberator crazy.

Revisiting an example may help to clarify the differences between these three forms of evaluation in practical reasoning. Consider again the person deciding whether to move to the US from the UK to further her career. One way of approaching this decision would be through quantitative calculation: given that the move would further

her career more than staying, and given that she values her career, the person should, all else being equal, move to the US. But consider – as is common in such decisions – how she should deliberate if all else is not equal. Imagine that she has ageing parents in the UK, whom she loves and who have cared for her well. Staying within the perspective of quantitative assessment, the person might compare the value of satisfying her desire to be loyal to the parents she loves with the value of satisfying her desire for a successful career. But it is hard to see what could count as a master-value according to which these desires can be compared, unless it is something like the sheer thrill or pleasure of having a desire satisfied. Quantitative assessment according to a master-value like this does not seem appropriate for such a decision.[8]

Another possibility is that the person avoids reductivist comparisons of the value of each choice and adopts instead a weakly evaluative perspective instead of embarking on a quantitative assessment as laid out in the last paragraph. Here, each option is valuable to the person, but both cannot be pursued, and they cannot be compared in terms of a master-value. In that case, her eventual choice might be a result of thinking about each option in its own terms, and choosing on the basis of something other than how the values embodied in each option contrast or cohere with her conception of herself. For example, she might toss a coin, ask a friend to decide for her, or wear a blindfold and throw a dart at a board where black represents going and red represents staying. Because the two options cannot be compared and neither – we are stipulating – impinges on or could articulate her self-conception, this way of choosing seems appropriate.

However, we would think that a person approaching a choice like this in such a way either did not really care about either of the options, or had failed to appreciate the importance of that choice. We would think that a person who, for example, tosses a coin to make such a decision does not really love her family or care about her career very much, because commitment to these things should make the choice between them more difficult. Of course, she genuinely may not care about the two options. But if she says she does, then the choice between them, we think, should be, if not agonised over, then at least taken seriously enough for the person to reflect on what commitment to each value means for commitment to the other, and which of them provides a reason for acting which is the sort of reason she takes to be appropriate for a person such as herself. When such clashes occur, should a loving daughter put her career on the back burner? Or can love still be expressed and familial obligation performed across oceans? When a person deliberates over options in this way, she tries to untangle what she thinks about the relation between them, and she does this in the light of her conception of herself. In other words, the questions just listed are asked in the *first-person*: should I privilege my career over caring for my parents? Does that make me a bad daughter? The person here tries to understand what is involved in *her* being a good daughter, and *her* successful pursuit of a career, not what is involved in successfully pursuing a career, by considering whether and how social standards of 'good daughterhood' (whatever these are) apply to her, given the details of her situation: her relationship with her parents, the expectations on both sides, the history of her career development, etc. As we saw in the last chapter, these sorts of considerations are self-respect related: when seeking self-respect, a person tries to succeed according to individual criteria of excellence, which map excellence for her in the activities and pursuits she cares about. In making this choice, the daughter's values may reflect social standards (if any there be) relating to what a good daughter does when faced with such a choice. Or her standards may diverge from social standards. The point is that, whatever the convergence or divergence, the daughter strongly evaluates by reflecting on standards which are *hers*, which form part of her conception of herself and which inform her self-respect.

Not all strongly evaluative deliberation will be over options which are, as in the example just given, practically incompatible: not all such deliberations will have a tragic aspect. Some strongly evaluative deliberation will be over options both of which it is possible for the person to pursue, but one of which is unacceptable, given the grounds of her self-respect. Furthermore, putting practically incommensurable problems in strongly evaluative terms does not make them easier to solve. However, that is not the point. Rather, making room for the category of strong evaluation captures the sense in which we attribute significance to some choices and not others. Choosing to go to America or to stay in the UK is not usually like the choice between an eclair or a *mille feuilles* from a pastry tray: it usually has more significance than that.[9] If such a choice is understood in terms of strong evaluation, its significance is explained – in large part – by the way in which each option is connected to, and would affect, the self-understanding of the person, and the future development of her character.

Strong evaluation is a matter of the contrastive assessment of reasons in a 'vocabulary of worth' generated by, and dependent upon, a person's self-respect.[10] If, as I shall argue, strong evaluation is what characterises the practical reasoning of people facing problems of justice, and if congruence is necessary for acquiring the vocabulary of worth used in strong evaluation, then we must assume that persons have self-respect if we are to think of them as capable of solving problems of justice through the use of practical reason. Let me start by outlining how congruence provides the vocabulary of worth necessary for strong evaluation.

Congruence is a matter of success according to individual criteria of excellence: such success strengthens a person's conception of herself as a particular sort of person. Conversely, when a person fails according to these criteria her conception of herself as a the sort of person for whom these criteria are appropriate receives a blow. But people are not born with ready-made self-conceptions. A person develops and retains a self-conception by doing things. People engage in projects, develop values, embark on relationships, accept and demand commitments, and strive towards goals: all of these activities can have self-respect related individual criteria of excellence associated with them. To the extent that a person succeeds according to these criteria she strengthens her conception of herself as a certain sort of person; that is, the sort of person for whom these criteria are appropriate.

It is according to a person's robust self-conception that reasons are contrastively assessed in strong evaluation. When evaluating in this way, a person asks herself whether acting for any of the reasons under evaluation contrasts with the self-conception generated by congruence, and at the heart of her self-respect (of course, she is unlikely to put it to herself in these terms). Given the diversity of self-conceptions fit to ground self-respect, reasons which are strongly evaluated in a positive light for a person with one sort of self-conception may not receive a positive evaluation by a person with another sort of self-conception: what counts as honourable for a thief may not count as honourable for a priest. The vocabulary of worth which characterises strong evaluation is informed by the self-conception of the person who uses it. Self-respect provides a context for strongly evaluative practical reasoning because a partial or total failure of congruence will destroy or damage a person's self-conception in such a way as to deprive her of the vocabulary of worth necessary for the strong evaluation of practical reasons. Let me examine in turn the effects of total and partial failures of congruence on strongly evaluative practical reasoning.

When a person's failure of congruence is total, she loses all sense of who she is and what she stands for: she no longer has any vocabulary of worth for practical reasoning. If I fail according to all the standards that matter to me, where I value these standards and think of them as worth having, and I believe that they reflect my abilities and ambitions, then my sense of who I am – what I am capable of, what I really care about and value, the shape my life has taken and will take – will disintegrate.[11] There are various ways in which a person can find herself in this predicament, and it is never obvious that a person who has lost all congruence is to be held wholly, or even partly, responsible for this loss. Sometimes people with exceptionally demanding individual criteria of excellence can suffer a total loss of congruence: insecure perfectionists who lack any self-forgiveness, or obsessively competitive and driven people who measure their own worth according to the most demanding social criteria of excellence are examples of the type. Here, we might claim that the person has not tailored her self-respect affecting standards to her actual abilities and talents, and thus that the disintegration of the person's self-conception in the light of her damning judgements of herself according to these standards is not appropriate.[12] In other cases we might think that the person's standards are well-matched to her abilities, values and interests, but that something about her character or situation leaves her unable to meet these standards. People with addictions to alcohol and drugs, people with self-destructive tendencies, and people suffering from pathological weakness of the will can all be examples of this type.

These are extreme cases: here, a person loses the ability to judge whether an end or set of means is appropriate for her when she is making evaluatively significant choices by losing her sense of herself as a certain sort of person, and thus by losing any sense of what sorts of reasons are and are not motivationally acceptable to her. A person whose failure of congruence is so complete that her sense of who she is and what she stands for has disintegrated no longer has a vocabulary of worth with which to assess reasons supporting different sets of ends and means.[13]

When confronted with people who have lost a vocabulary of worth, and with it the ability to make strongly evaluative judgements in their practical reasoning, we have mixed feelings: pity, incomprehension, compassion, revulsion and relief that we ourselves have avoided such a fate are all common reactions. Such reactions reveal the importance we attribute to that which is lost by people who have totally lost congruence; that is, a vocabulary of worth for strong evaluation. Of course, people who have lost congruence have often also lost their family, friends and career. But these losses can in many cases be explained in terms of how the damaged person ceases to be recognisable as the person she was to friends and family who want to offer support, or in terms of how she ceases to function effectively in her career path. The loss of congruence prompting these other losses is often signalled by those who turn away from the damaged person when they say that the person is no longer herself, or that they no longer recognise her.

That congruence provides a context for strongly evaluative practical reasoning is most clear in stark and tragic cases of a total loss of congruence. But it is also apparent in less dramatic cases where congruence is damaged rather than lost completely. A person with a robust self-conception supported through secure congruence has advantages with respect to strong evaluation over a person whose self-conception is fragile in virtue of limited or damaged congruence. The difference between them relates to the *quality* of the vocabulary of worth they bring to their practical reasoning. A person with a robust self-conception has a vocabulary of worth of a greater depth and articulacy than a person with a fragile self-conception. A person whose congruence supports her confidence in her abilities to pursue her plans, and her assurance that these plans are the right ones for her, possesses the capacity to make more fine-grained and resolute strong evaluations of reasons than a person whose limited congruence leaves her plagued by self-doubt and the spectre of regret for a life ill-planned. A person with a robust self-conception is able to make strong evaluations with conviction, because she is sure that, being *this* sort of person, certain reasons are base and dishonourable, or noble and honourable. A person with a fragile self-conception is not in a position to make such resolute assessments; her assessments of reasons will be more tentative and unsure. This is perhaps why adolescents, who are normally only just beginning to develop a robust self-conception, can switch backwards and forwards between different sets of strong evaluations. The person with a fragile self-conception will, as it were, always be looking back over her shoulder in the process of strongly evaluative practical reasoning, wondering if her assessments are correct or her judgement is really sound.

The argument of this section has been that non-subservience provides a context for justice-oriented practical reasoning, and that congruence provides a context for strongly evaluative practical reasoning. If it can be shown that practical reasoning about justice is strongly evaluative then congruence provides a context for such reasoning, in which case self-respect as a whole is an idea of practical reason as it faces problems of justice. I turn to this in the next section.

4.3   Practical reason for justice-seekers

Why should we think that practical reasoning about justice must be strongly evaluative? Consider first what justice-justification would have to be like if its success depended on the possibility of accepting reasons through the use of practical reason as quantitative calculation. When practical reasoning takes this form, reasons are assessed in terms of the extent to which the options they support promote a unitary value or good, such as utility. If a set of principles are taken to be justified in virtue of the claim that it is impossible for persons to reject them after quantitative calculation, then it must be the case that these persons are assumed to share the value or a commitment to the good in terms of which the calculation takes place. But we cannot attribute this thought to stage 2 persons given that we seek an explanation of why it is that they accept the permanence of pluralism with respect to these questions.

One version of the quantitative approach which might seem more attractive takes the value to which all people are committed to be their own welfare. This has more initial plausibility than the utilitarian approach just considered if an account of welfare is given in terms of preference- or desire-satisfaction, and if maximisation is presented as the strategy that each person adopts *within* her own life, rather than the strategy that the state should adopt *across* persons' lives. It might be argued that quantitative assessment understood in this way is appropriate with respect to practical reasoning about principles of justice: it is appropriate for a person to reject principles which do not ensure for her maximum satisfaction of her desires or preferences, or which do not compensate her when she cannot achieve maximum satisfaction.

It is certainly the case that quantitative assessment understood in terms of individual welfare maximisation is sometimes appropriate in practical reasoning. When a person chooses a walk on the beach at night rather than during the day because it will give her more of a thrill to walk at night, or champagne over cider because it gives a better quality sense of giddiness, she does not reason inappropriately. Given that a person prefers the sound of the sea at night over its sound during the day, or desires quality giddiness, there is nothing wrong with her aiming to maximise satisfaction of these preferences or desires in her life. But is this acceptable as a picture of what people aim at when they choose principles of justice? Remembering the claim that stage 2 people achieve self-respect in a diversity of ways, and accept this diversity as a permanent fact about their constituency of justification, the claim that quantitative assessment is appropriate in practical reasoning about justice has an unwelcome implication. If this claim is true, then all the diverse commitments which people bring to their practical reasoning about principles of justice should be understood on the individual welfare maximisation model, otherwise the non-satisfaction of preferences or desires would not be appropriate as grounds on which principles could be rejected. In other words, each of these commitments should be thought of as valued by and important to the person who has them because each commitment is constituted by a set of desires and preferences, of which the person wants to satisfy as many as possible.

A conception of persons as preference- or desire-satisfaction maximisers in their practical reasoning about *all* their commitments and decisions is unacceptable. Ronald Dworkin characterises preference-satisfaction maximisers as 'buzz addicts': their practical reasoning aims at the maximisation of 'emotional highs or buzzes' through certain experiences which the buzz addicts call 'preferences'.[14] He characterises desire-satisfaction maximisers as 'tick addicts': their practical reasoning is driven by the aim 'to tick off as many instances as possible of "desire-satisfaction"', where a tick addict's desire is just what she happens to find that she wants.[15] Dworkin claims that if we were buzz- or tick-addicts we would view preferences which are expensive to satisfy, and desires which are hard to fulfil, as impediments to the achievement of buzzes or the scoring of ticks; we would think of such preferences and desires as handicaps that we have, and we would want to substitute them for more easily satisfiable preferences and desires, so as to maximise our buzz and tick scores. Dworkin rightly rejects this picture of our practical reasoning. Many of the preferences and desires that we have are saturated with judgements about the value of what is preferred or desired: 'If you love jazz, it is jazz that you love, not some sensation that you happen to realise at a jazz concert but that you might hope to obtain in some different and perhaps less expensive way.'[16]

Conceiving of members of the constituency of justification as individual welfare-maximisers is tantamount to conceiving of them as buzz- and tick-addicts. Rather, that a person has the preferences and desires she does is to be explained in terms of her conception of the preferences and desires which are appropriate for a person such as herself to retain self-respect. But in that case, and going beyond Dworkin's argument, that a person has certain desires and preferences is irrelevant to establishing the grounds on which she could reject justificatory reasons. What matters instead is how those reasons cohere or contrast with the values at the heart of her self-conception, and the extent to which they will create social conditions in which it is possible for her to act congruently with her self-conception, and thus preserve it. But when a person's practical reasoning proceeds in this way she is a strong evaluator: her preferences and desires – whether or not they are understood as mere instruments for the accumulation of buzzes and ticks – do not provide the ultimate grounds for the possible rejection of justificatory reasons.

Next, consider the implications of conceiving of justice-oriented practical reasoning as weakly evaluative. When a person weakly evaluates competing options she values but cannot have both, and the value she attaches to each option lacks significance for her; this is why it is acceptable for weak evaluators to justify their choices by saying, 'I just felt like it', or 'the mood took me'. Could practical reasoning about principles of justice be like this? Could justificatory success be defeated by persons who reject principles because they just feel like it? If this is the case, then it seems that no justificatory reasons could ever succeed: it is always possible for any person to reject any principle just because the mood takes her. The kind of reasoning that we need to think of persons as engaging in in order to gauge whether principles are impossible for them to reject has to have more depth and articulacy than this: it has to be strongly evaluative.

Earlier I considered some examples of decisions for which weakly evaluating and quantitatively assessing practical reasoning seemed inappropriate. The reason why is that each of the examples stipulated that the decision in question has evaluative significance for the person making it; in each example the person was described as being committed to both of the values, expressed as reasons for action, between which she has to decide. But there was no suggestion that all persons ought to be committed to the stipulated values of love for parents, commitment to a career, passion for equality, concern for one's child etc. For some people, weak evaluation with respect to decisions involving these values may be appropriate: not all parents are worthy of love, not all careers are fulfilling and rewarding, and not all children are worth the sacrifice of moral commitments. So why is thinking about principles of justice different? There are two questions here. (1) Why should we think that practical reasoning about questions of justice is strongly evaluative at all?; (2) Why think that the choice of principles of justice has evaluative significance for all people, rather than just for those who care about such principles? Let me turn to the first question first.

When a person strongly evaluates a reason she considers what it would mean for her conception of herself as a certain sort of person were she to be motivated to act for that reason. My claim has been that what it is for a person to have the robust self-conception making strong evaluation possible is for her to have self-respect. Given these claims, a characterisation of justice-oriented practical reasoning as strongly evaluative may strike some people as odd. Is it really the case that when a person thinks about where revenue from tax can best be spent she in some way consults her self-conception? Or, is it plausible that when a person thinks about reasons for and against permitting GM foods trials that her self-respect is somehow implicated in this assessment?

In cases like these it is not plausible that a person's self-respect must be involved in her justificatory reasoning (although, of course, it might be); but then, it is not plausible that these are cases of strong evaluation at all. Rather, they might be cases of quantitative calculation. But if this is so, isn't my account of justice-oriented practical reasoning as strongly evaluative scuppered? It is not, because the cases just considered need not be thought of as involving questions of basic justice, and it is only with respect to these cases that practical reasoning is strongly evaluative.[17] When we consider assessments of reasons relating to questions of basic justice, the claim that self-respect is implicated in these assessments looks more plausible. For example, when a liberal person rejects justificatory reasons for denying opportunities for education and employment to black people, she does so on the grounds that, being committed to equality and the moral arbitrariness of skin colour, such a reason cannot be endorsed by her. Importantly, this is *not* tantamount to the claim that all that matters to a person in her assessment of justificatory reasons is that her own self-conception is protected. The liberal person's rejection of racist reasons is not a form of moral narcissism or evaluative navel-gazing. Rather, the liberal person rejects racist reasons because she is committed – in a way connected to her self-respect – to equality for all, which means she is committed to equality for black people: she has a self-respect related commitment to securing justice *for them*.

Turning to the second question, we can see this should be treated as analogous to the question about the amoralist in moral philosophy. The amoralist is a person who recognises the existence of the demands of morality, recognises that they apply to other people, but denies that they apply to her.[18] The possible existence of such a person who has the same attitude to the requirement to engage in political justification as the amoralist has to moral requirements is what gives rise to the question. I suspect that, just as there is nothing that we can say to the amoralist to get her to accept the requirements of morality, so there is nothing we can say to a person who claims that political justification is avoidable for her. But the fact that we cannot say anything to such a person does not mean that there is nothing we can say about her, and what we can say about her reveals the costs of the claim that political justification is avoidable. Because this is not a book about the unavoidability of political justification, but rather starts from the assumption that justification is unavoidable, I shall not discuss the second question any further here.

The claims I have argued for so far in this chapter are as follows.

(1) Justice-oriented practical reasoning is strongly evaluative.
(2) Strong evaluation requires self-respect. If we combine this with the assumption that political justification is unavoidable, i.e. that all person are committed to searching for solutions to their shared problems of justice, then we get:
(3) Persons engaged in strongly evaluative justificatory debate about problems of justice must be assumed to have, and to care about, their self-respect and its social conditions. Self-respect is an idea of practical reason as it faces problems of justice.

It might be objected that even if (1)–(3) are accepted, this does not entail that self-respecting justice-seekers will be able to find solutions to their problems of justice, either in the form of procedures for justificatory debate, or in the form of substantive principles of justice (which may or may not issue from such procedures). This problem arises given the fact that the self-conceptions informing self-respect are deeply diverse. If we take deep diversity seriously, why should we expect that each practical reasoner arriving at a conception of justice through strong evaluation will come to any form of agreement about procedures for justificatory debate, or substantive principles? From the fact that all persons are united in the evaluative significance they attach to the choice of principles of justice *per se* it does not follow that they will all make the same choices through strongly evaluative practical reasoning. This is because each person's self-respect is informed by different values, commitments, and standards. If strong evaluation is the hallmark of practical reasoning about justice, and strong evaluation is tied to self-respect, can any justificatory reasons succeed? And are these reasons really less demanding than those required by the incommensurability and burdens interpretations of the permanence of pluralism? I address these questions in sections 4.4 and 4.5 respectively.

4.4 Self-respect, civility and public reason

My claim at the end of Chapter 2 was that a minimally demanding Constructivist procedure of justification can be yielded once we characterise stage 2 ideal people as accepting the permanence of pluralism as a consequence of their acceptance that all persons care about their own self-respect. But this will only be of interest to liberal Constructivists if it can be shown that a person's commitment to her self-respect and its social conditions, combined with an acknowledgement that all other people share these commitments, can be shown to yield commitment to principles of toleration and procedures of public reason, in the sense that reasons for practising toleration and endorsing public reason could not be rejected by self-respecting people. In this section I make that argument.

In what follows I shall take it that commitment to procedures of public reason entails commitment to toleration. So if an argument can be made to show that self-respecting ideal people could not reject reasons to engage in public reasoning, then this argument also shows that they could not reject reasons to practice toleration. The scope of public reason – that is, the constituency of people with whom public reasoning is appropriate – maps the limits of toleration.[19] All others with whom a person is committed to engaging with in public reason governed debate she is also committed to tolerating. Toleration requires a person's principled refusal to use force or coercion to change the views of others, where she has reason to disapprove of these views. To be in a position to engage in public reason with another person therefore requires toleration of that person. If a person is committed to solving problems of justice with all others through the use of public reason then she is committed to tolerating the views of all others, as a precondition of such engagement. In what follows my argument will focus upon establishing that the people who accept the permanence of pluralism in virtue of the significance of self-respect could not reject reasons to endorse public reason: this establishes that they could not reject reasons to practice toleration as well. (Note that the failure of this argument would not signal the failure of a parallel argument for toleration: that those who care about their own self-respect and recognise that others do so too could reject reasons to engage in public reasoning does not establish that they could reject reasons to practice toleration. However, I think the argument for public reasoning succeeds, and so there is no need to make the remedial argument for toleration.)

Let me start by recapping on the ideal of public reason. Given the unavoidability of political justification, and the fact of deep diversity, a person engaged in justificatory debate who simply asserts her own strongly evaluative views about the correct solution to problems of justice as decisive does not offer others reasons fit to justify her proposals *to them*. As Rawls remarks, 'public justification is not simply valid reasoning, but argument *addressed to others*'.[20] If deep diversity is permanent, all persons accept this, and all persons are assumed to be self-respecters, then no person can expect others to strongly evaluate justificatory reasons with a vocabulary of worth identical to her own. Accepting the fact of deep diversity means accepting that self-respect can be achieved according to a plurality of individual criteria of excellence, and thus that each self-respecter will strongly evaluate justificatory reasons in a different way. In that case, any self-respecting person engaged in justificatory debate under these conditions must offer others justificatory reasons which she sincerely and genuinely takes to be reasons that others could accept as justificatory reasons through strong evaluation in a vocabulary of worth informed by their self-respect. In other words, self-respecters who bring their strong evaluations to public justification are committed to the use of public reason when engaging with other self-respecters in justificatory debates about problems of justice. This does not mean that justificatory reasons must always be presented in public reason in the first instance. As Rawls' 'proviso' allows, these reasons can initially be presented as thick, comprehensive reasons indexed to, and expressed in terms of, a particular conception of the good. But so long as these reasons are eventually presented in public reason they are appropriate as justificatory reasons.[21]

Rawls' account of the ideal of public reason can be adapted to reflect assumptions about the self-respect of justice-seekers, as follows.

(1) Public officials – judges, legislators, candidates for public office, etc. – present their political justifications to citizens in terms of reasons which they sincerely and genuinely take to be reasons which the public, and other officials, could endorse through their strongly evaluative practical reasoning.[22]

(2) Ordinary citizens 'view themselves as ideal legislators' in order to judge whether public officials satisfy (1), and do what they can to criticise and remove from office public officials who fail to satisfy (1).[23]

(3) Ordinary citizens are willing and able to offer to one another only those justificatory reasons which they sincerely and genuinely take to be reasons that each could accept as justificatory reasons

through strong evaluation, given that they accept that their self-respect related differences are permanent, which means that they will permanently differ with respect to the vocabulary of worth they bring to strong evaluation.[24]

Conditions (1)–(3) lay out an ideal of public justification for self-respecting strong evaluators. Given their commitment to finding some procedures for the solution of problems of justice, their commitment to their own self-respect, and the acceptance that each of them differs with respect to the vocabulary of worth they use to evaluate justificatory reasons then – if they are to offer one another reasons at all – they cannot offer one another reasons which could only be accepted by others using the same vocabulary of worth, for example, reasons steeped in religious tradition, or reasons indexed to clan or tribe membership. Instead, a person's justifcatory reasons must be taken by her to be acceptable to others who differ in the personal bases of their self-respect, but who are as committed to their self-respect as she is to hers.

Why is it the case that a commitment to self-respect, and an acknowledgement of a similar commitment on the part of others entails a commitment to public reason? A possible objection here is that a person's commitment to her own self-respect is in tension with a commitment to public reason and toleration of the social conditions of self-respect for others. How can it be that a person whose self-respect is staked upon her Catholicism, and the family values it contains, can tolerate Gay Pride marches in London, let alone engage in public reasoning with those who go on these marches? There are two ways to make this objection. First, it might be argued that the exercise of public reason requires qualities and involves the exercise of skills which self-respecters cannot be expected to have. Or second, it might be argued that the motivation to endorse public reason is in conflict with the motivation to acquire and maintain self-respect. If either of these objections succeeds then self-respecters could not accept reasons to engage in public reasoning, in which case it is not true that self-respecters could not reject reasons to engage in public reasoning, and the minimally demanding Constructivist procedure fails (at least with respect to the liberal ideal of public reason). Let me start with the first objection.

Justificatory debate in public reason requires that a person have the following qualities and exercise the following skills.

- The ability to discern when another person's beliefs, values, wants and commitments differ from her own.
- The ability to tell how others differ from her by listening to their self-descriptions, and the terms of their vocabulary of worth, so as to be able to judge whether her strongly evaluative justificatory reasons are presentable in public reason to these other people.
- The capacity for empathy, enabling the person to imagine what it would be like for another self-respecting person to be presented with the strongly evaluative reasons which she proposes as justificatory reasons.
- An acceptance of the possibility that she might be mistaken about the extent to which her strongly evaluative reasons are in fact presentable in public reason.[25] Without this, there is no possibility that any person can be brought to change her mind about solutions to problems of justice through justificatory discourse, whether or not it is framed in terms of public reason.
- Sincerity in the presentation of justificatory reasons in public reason: the reasons a person claims to sincerely and genuinely believe to be presentable in public reason must really be believed by her to have this character. Without sincerity, the whole procedure of public justification can become a sham disguising the machinations of those competing for power behind the scenes of fake justificatory procedures.

When a person exercises these skills in relation to others, and does so so as to engage in justificatory debate governed by the idea of public reason, she meets what Rawls calls her 'duty of civility'. The current objection, then, is that we cannot expect self-respecters to be civil, in which case they cannot be expected to construct procedures of justification governed by the ideal of public reason. Instead, we might conceive of justificatory discourses between self-respecters in terms of a contest of full-blooded, comprehensive reasons, all of which are presented as expressing correct or true values.[26]

In response, a conception of persons as self-respecters does not require a conception of political justification as a contest of reasons; at least, not in virtue of the claim that self-respecters must lack the civility necessary for engagement in public reason. By tracing connections between the search for self-respect in associational life and acquisition of the attributes of civility, the first objection – that self-respecting persons *ipso facto* will lack the qualities and skills necessary for engagement in public reason – is met.

We saw in the last chapter that self-respect depends on the formation of a non-subservient self-conception which includes individual criteria of excellence for the activities central to this self-conception: self-respect is maintained when a person succeeds according to these criteria. Rawls gives an account of the development of individual criteria of excellence in terms of the Aristotelian principle which, once properly understood as divested of any perfectionist implications, states that, the more success a person has according to her individual criteria, the more demanding and complex these criteria will become.

What matters from the point of view of responding to the objection is what Rawls calls the 'companion effect' to the Aristotelian principle. This is that,

> As we witness the exercise of the well-trained abilities of others, these displays are enjoyed by us and arouse a desire that we should be able to do the same things ourselves. We want to be like those persons who can exercise the abilities we find latent in our nature.[27]

The companion effect to the Aristotelian principle introduces a social element into the account of self-respect in two ways. First, for a person to be in a position to witness displays of talent and so be prompted to emulate these displays herself usually requires some form of association with others. This association need not be formal, overly intimate, or especially prolonged. But it must be close enough for the person to witness the exercise of others' well-trained abilities, and the effect they have on others. Second, satisfying the Aristotelian principle matters for self-respect because such satisfaction is likely to prompt the esteem and respect of others, and a person's receipt of the esteem and respect of others is conducive to her respecting and esteeming herself. Again, association need not be formal, intimate, or prolonged, but only close enough for others to witness the person's display of talent and so experience the companion effect for themselves. When associations play these roles they provide a person with the conditions of reciprocal esteem I described as associational bases of self-respect in the last chapter. Involvement in communities of shared interests providing the associational bases of self-respect requires that a person acquire the qualities and exercise the skills of civility for the following reasons.

A person's association with others in pursuit of self-respect requires that she be accepted by those others. Acceptance can take the form of anything from formal initiation to mere tolerance of the person's presence, either of which are adequate for observing the exercise of developed talents and experiencing the companion effect. But even in an association in which co-operative activity is central to membership, participation is well-defined, and the bonds of shared beliefs and values are strong, there will nevertheless be differences between associates, who are never clones of one another. This means that a prospective associate must adapt her behaviour in different ways for different extant associates, which requires that she gauge the extent to which, and way in which, each member's point of view differs from her own. This involves the acquisition and exercise of two key skills of civility: acknowledgement of difference, and the ability to listen to others so as to judge how they differ.[28]

Gaining the self-respect related benefits of the conditions of reciprocal esteem not only depends on the fact of a person's association with others, but also depends on her learning from established members so as to emulate them and prompt the esteem of her newly acquired peers. This means that a person must be open to the possibility that the views and values she brings to association with like-minded others may be changed through association with them. Without such openness, a person cannot learn. For some people, this openness will be a result of their accepting that their own judgement is burdened, and thus that their commitment to views and values generated by this judgement may change when they are exposed to others who have exercised their judgement differently. But, importantly, this need not be the case for all persons seeking support for their self-respect in associational life. There are various reasons why such people might be open to being changed by association with others in the pursuit of self-respect. In many cases, for example, established members of communities of reciprocal esteem may be regarded as masters or experts in virtue of their epistemic or spiritual access to the truth with respect to the values in question. In other cases, established members may simply be regarded as more practised in that around which the community is organised, in the sense of having clocked up more years doing what it is the community does.

When a person is involved in a community of shared interests she hopes to be able to exhibit skills and talents which both satisfy her own criteria of excellence for the activities of the community, and which also elicit the appreciation, respect, and esteem of others. In order to gauge whether her performances will achieve this a self-respecting person has to be able to empathise with other members of the group, so as to gain an idea of what things look like from where they stand, and so how her performance would look to them.

The final attribute of civility necessary for engagement in public reason is sincerity in the presentation of reasons to others. This capacity is, again, intimately connected with participation in a community of shared interests. This is because, first, it would be a waste of time for a self-respecter to attempt to participate in a community whose activities she did not sincerely value in terms of her self-respect: the very fact of involvement in such communities means that a person has experience of what it is to be sincerely committed to certain values, and to communicate this commitment to others through speech and action. And second, even if a person were to non-sincerely involve herself in a community of shared interests, for whatever reasons, it is unlikely that her lack of sincerity would go undetected by other members of the community for long. Persons who are genuinely committed to certain activities and values are generally skilled at spotting the signs of commitment in others, and a person lacking sincerity would likely find herself unwelcome in any community of shared interests in which she attempted to participate.

The claim that to benefit from association with others a person must realise that their views differ in part from hers, must be sensitive to these differences, must be empathetic towards them in order to gain the self-respect related benefits of association with them, and must furthermore sincerely value what they value to gain these benefits, has intuitive appeal. A person who arrogantly talks over others, ignores their views, fails to recognise their differences and so insults and offends them, or participates in their activities as a means to some end other than the maintenance and development of her self-respect, will not find a social basis of self-respect in such associations, and is likely to find herself excluded from them.[29] Of course, some groups will lack civility altogether. Groups whose members abuse, humiliate or dictate to one another are not schools for civility: but neither are they schools for self-respect, which depends on a person maintaining a sense of her own status, and having the opportunity to act in accordance with her individual criteria of excellence. In that case such groups do not stand as counterexamples to the claim that membership of a self-respect supporting group requires the acquisition and exercise of the skills of civility, because such groups aim to undermine some members' sense of their own status, and deny them opportunity to achieve congruence.

In sum, once the nature of the communities of shared interests providing the associational bases of self-respect is made clear, we can see that most self-respecters will have acquired the skills and qualities necessary for civility through participation in these communities. Thus, it is wrong to think that a person's commitment to her self-respect is in tension with acquiring the attributes necessary for engaging in justificatory debate governed by the ideal of public reason. The beauty of tracing connections between self-respect and civility through the associational bases of self-respect is that it does not imply that persons capable of civility have virtuous dispositions, especially good intentions, or uniform attitudes towards the exercise of their own judgement: all it requires is that they care about their own self-respect.

However, the second version of the objection that self-respect provides no grounds for endorsing public reason is still to be met. This objection is that, even if a person has acquired the attributes of civility, her commitment to her self-respect is in tension with her endorsement of justificatory debate according to the ideal of public reason. Although the response to the first objection showed that self-respecting people are *capable* of civility in their interaction with others in their communities of shared interests, it has not been shown that self-respecting persons have a reason to extend civility to other self-respecters outside of their communities of shared interests, and to engage with them in public reason. The objection is that the commitment to public reasoning in deep diversity conflicts with commitments which are part and parcel of having self-respect: a motivational commitment to public reasoning in political justification is in tension with a motivational commitment to self-respect.[30]

There are two ways to understand this criticism. The first is: a self-respecting person *has a reason not to engage in public reason*, because such engagement demands that she relinquish the commitments which inform her self-respect. The second is: a self-respecting person *has no reason to engage in public reason*, because such engagement brings her no self-respect related benefits. I shall address each of these versions in turn. Providing responses to them – especially the second version – supplies the connection between self-respect and public reason that is needed if the many flowers interpretation of the permanence of pluralism can yield a minimally demanding Constructivism.

The first version of the objection fails because it trades on a misconception of public reasoning as a form of denial, or amnesia. Public reasoning does not require of a person that she somehow pretend that she lacks the values and commitments at the heart of her self-respect, or that she try to forget, deny, or abrogate her self-respect related commitments when engaging in justificatory discourse. Public reasoning does not require that a person repudiate the self-conception at the heart of her self-respect. All it asks of a person is that she sincerely consider whether the strongly evaluative reasons informed by her self-respect could serve as reasons for others with different vocabularies of worth, just as sincerely held. If a person sincerely believes that her strongly evaluative reasons pass this test, then these reasons are admissible in justificatory debate, and she has performed her duty of civility. Far from asking people to deny their most fundamental beliefs, or distance themselves from their commitments, public reason requires that people explore these commitments and beliefs so as to assess which of them might serve as public reasons in civil justificatory debate. A person alienated from all her self-respect related commitments would be unable to engage in public reason. Civility and public reason is defeated by anomie and apathy, not by the commitments at the heart of self-respect.

Let me turn now to the second version of the objection, which is that a self-respecting person *has no reason to engage in public reason*, because such engagement brings her no self-respect related benefits. I shall isolate two responses to this, both of which show that a minimally demanding self-respect based Constructivism yields liberal results, but each of which has different consequences for the extent to which those who care about their self-respect and acknowledge that others do so too are committed to actively engaging in public reasoning. The first response is that political society as a whole is an associational basis of self-respect, which means that a failure to engage in public reasoning with others members of this association damages the reciprocal esteem characteristic of these associations, and thus damages the self-respect of those who so refuse. The second response does not rely on such a controversial conception of political society. Rather, the argument here will be that the unavoidability of problems of justice, combined with the fact that political institutions distribute the social bases of self-respect, means each person has an interest in (at least) not sabotaging or attempting to undermine procedures of political justification governed by the ideal of public reason, even if no person has a reason to be actively and frequently engaged in public reason.

Remarks suggestive of the first response can be found in Rawls.

> [T]he reason why [the duty of civility] would be acknowledged is that although the parties in the original position take no interest in each other's interests, they know that in society they need to be assured by the esteem of their associates. Their self-respect and their confidence in the value of their own system of ends cannot withstand the indifference much less the contempt of others. Everyone benefits from living in a society where the duty of mutual respect is honoured. The cost to self-interest is minor in comparison with the support for a sense of one's own worth.[31]

We can use Rawls' claim about political society as supportive of self-respect to argue that a failure to engage in public reasoning will undermine the conditions of self-respect for those who fail by making them subject to the harsh judgements of their fellow citizens. If this is the case then self-respecters do have a reason for engaging in public reasoning, and for exercising the skills of civility in their dealings with others not intimately associated with them in communities of shared interests.

This response makes self-respect sensitive to the judgements of others with whom the self-respecting person may have nothing in common except shared membership of a political society. Is this plausible? Consider what it is that a person who rejects public reasoning in justificatory debate with others is refusing to do. First, she refuses to consider whether her reasons could serve as reasons for others, and instead presents them in their full-blooded comprehensiveness: in deep diversity, this just appears to others as the person insisting on her own beliefs simply because they are her own beliefs. Second, the person does not listen to others when they disagree with her views, perhaps insisting that, deep down, they do not really disagree with her. In that case there is no reason for her to attempt to empathise with other people: all she need do is consult how her reasons would strike her were they presented to her by another person. This will strike others as insufferably patronising. Third, the person refuses to admit that she may be wrong about whether her reasons are presentable in public reason. This will appear to others as the height of arrogance. And finally, given the person's attitudes towards her own beliefs, if she does engage with others in justificatory debate, she may insincerely claim that she genuinely takes the reasons she presents them with to be reasons which they too could accept. Given that such a person believes herself to have access to the whole truth, she may feel that such insincerity is justified as a way of maximising the odds that the principles she endorses become dominant. This will strike others as sneaky and manipulative.

Admittedly, this is the worst case scenario of a person who fails on all counts with respect to public reason and the duty of civility. Such a person will be judged by her fellow self-respecting citizens to be patronising, arrogant, manipulative and sneaky. These sorts of judgement give those who make them a reason to avoid those they judge. In particular, they have a reason to avoid justificatory debate with such people over matters as important as principles of basic justice. In that case, a person who rejects public reason and refuses to exercise the skills of civility excludes herself from justificatory debate with others; her reasons as they stand will not be not taken into account when it comes to solving problems of justice. Such a person's awareness that others with whom she unavoidably stands shoulder to shoulder in facing problems of justice are not willing to consider her reasons in their conversations about how to solve these problems can lead her to question the vocabulary of worth in which her reasons are expressed. The person may well continue to excel according to her own criteria of excellence, but if such success takes place against the background of doubt about the values informing these criteria – even where this is toughed out as a defiant 'I don't care' attitude – then her self-respect can be damaged. And this will also be the case, even if to a lesser extent, with respect to persons who fail in only some of the ways mentioned. (Of course, there are some people whose self-respect is impervious to the negative judgements of others, but such people will be rare.)

But what if a person who refuses to engage in public reason has the support of her community of shared interests to fall back on? What if, given this support, the harsh judgements of her fellow citizens are like water off a duck's back when it comes to her self-respect? Unless the other members of this community are similarly contemptuous of public reasoning, they will, in addition to being members of this particular community, also be members of political society as a whole, with whom the person stands shoulder to shoulder in facing problems of justice. In which case, we might think that the person's community of shared interests will provide her with no hiding place from the harsh judgements of her fellow citizens.

But what if such a community is united in its rejection of public reasoning? What if all of its members stand shoulder to shoulder with one another, in opposition to the rest of political society, which is united on procedures of public reason? These groups are the hard cases for the argument because they seem to provide individual members who reject public reason with sufficient associational support for their self-respect to enable them to withstand the withdrawal of the associational support available in the judgements and responses of fellow self-respecting citizens, who are not members of that particular association.

One way of responding to these cases is to claim that such communities of shared interests do not, in fact, serve as associational bases of self-respect, either because they rely on the subservience of their members for their continued existence and success, or because they do not really provide their members with the opportunity to pursue their individual criteria of excellence. This response is inadequate because although this may be true of some such groups – for example, hierarchical religious cults – this cannot be assumed to be true of all such groups.

The second response is to admit that such groups can provide associational support for self-respect, but weaken the idea of what is involved in being committed to public reason. The weaker claim is that although self-respect does not necessarily commit the self-respecter to engagement in public reason herself, it nevertheless commits her to not interfering with public reason governed procedures of justification, or with public reason governed debate amongst others. In other words, the weaker position with respect to the endorsement of public reason is that although the self-respect of some people is consistent with their rejection of public reason for themselves, it is not consistent with their rejection of procedures of justification governed by public reason *per se*. In that case, members of groups which reject public reason for themselves can at most abstain from justificatory debate governed by the ideal of public reason and avoid engagement with others in these terms: what they cannot do is directly oppose such justificatory debate, or attempt to overthrow or replace it. The argument is as follows.

All people potentially face problems of justice which are connected with their access to the social bases of self-respect: there are no communities of reciprocal esteem which are beyond the reach of political influence, and so no group can claim that its values, organisation, and practices are permanently immune from political action and the outcome of justificatory debate. For all communities of shared interests, there is always the possibility that future changes of political principle or practice will diminish their effectiveness as sites of opportunity for self-respect for members. Furthermore, each individual member of a community of shared interests cannot be certain that that group will continue to provide her with a social basis of self-respect. Peoples' lives are full of surprises and unexpected developments. So even a person who is as certain as she can be that her group as it stands is unlikely to be diminished as a site of opportunity for self-respect through political action cannot be sure that she will never change and need to seek out groups whose provision of these opportunities is more threatened, or precarious. If people accept (1) that self-respect is necessary for anyone to reason practically about problems of justice, (2) that many different self-conceptions can provide the grounds for self-respect, given that they meet the non-subservience and congruence requirements, and (3) that political justification is unavoidable, then they must be committed to not interfering with the operation of public reason in procedures of political justification. Given the susceptibility of all communities of shared interests to political influence, and the permanent possibility that a person's self-respect supporting self-conception can change, those who presently reject public reason for themselves in the name of their self-respect cannot reject the adoption of procedures of political justification governed by public reason by their society as a whole. To reject these procedures by attempting to overturn them does two things which could become damaging to the future self-respect of those who reject public reason for themselves.

(1) It makes political justification a matter of establishing a *modus vivendi*. When procedures of justification are not governed by public reason, the values which will dominate political justification will be those of the group with the most power. As no group can be sure of continuing to be the most powerful group – and hence of continuing to have the loudest voice – any person for whom a group provides associational support for her self-respect cannot be committed to undermining procedures of justification governed by public reason. This commitment allows for the possibility that the group which currently provides her with opportunity for self-respect will be dismantled by a future group opposed to it which ascends to power and soaks public political justification with its own values. In that case, the person would lose her current associational bases of self-respect.

(2) The dynamics of self-respect – the way its personal bases can change and evolve over a life time – mean that no person can be sure that the group which currently provides her with associational bases of self-respect will continue to do so into the future. In that case, the attempt to undermine public reason governed procedures of political justification always runs the risk of excluding groups to which a person might want to turn for support for her self-respect in the future, thus endangering the possibility that these groups will be in a position to provide her with the conditions of reciprocal esteem should she need them.

The upshot of these considerations is that every self-respecting person has an interest in protecting procedures of justification governed by the ideal of public reason, even if not every person has a reason to engage actively in public reason herself. The commitment to public reason yielded by this argument is much weaker than the one yielded by a conception of political society as a whole as an associational basis of self-respect. But it is, nevertheless, a commitment to protect the sorts of justificatory procedures which characterise liberal thinking about political justification, and it has the advantage over the stronger argument that it does not rely on a controversial conception of political society. In any case, if either of these arguments is successful then the claim that conceiving of people at stage 2 as caring about their own self-respect and as acknowledging that others do so too means that reasons for endorsing public reason governed procedures of justification is vindicated.

4.5 Many flowers: demandingness revisited

The last two chapters have presented the materials required for a liberal Constructivist procedure of justification which is less demanding than similar procedures reliant on the incommensurability and the burdens views of the permanence of pluralism. It is time to pull the strands of these arguments together. Let me begin by recapping on the demandingness of the incommensurability and burdens views, and the problem faced by a liberal Constructivism which aims to rely on a less demanding explanation of why pluralism is taken to be an enduring fact by stage 2 persons.

Demandingness is a feature of justificatory reasons which is measured by considering how much uniformity would be required across a set of people in order for those people to accept the reasons. In Chapter 1 I briefly discussed various ways in which justificatory reasons can be demanding: belief, desire, motivation, and character. The language of measurement used here should not give the false impression that assessing demandingness is a precise science: it is not. The demandingness of a justificatory reason is a matter of judgement, and there are no hard and fast criteria which can be applied across all reasons: each case must be judged on its own merits. Questions of demandingness arise for externalist and deliberative internalist theories of the motivational adequacy of reasons, i.e. theories which state either that reasons can be motivationally adequate in the absence of an interesting connection with any of a person's present motivational commitments, or that the motivational adequacy of a reason is a matter of whether a person could come to acquire a motivational commitment to act for that reason by deliberating soundly from her present motivational commitments. Either way, most theories of political justification – including Constructivism – work with one of these conceptions of motivational adequacy, and so most of them face questions of demandingness.

Liberal constructivism as it is found in Rawls crucially relies on a conception of the person as accepting that pluralism is permanent: it is to such people (who, of course, have all the other characteristics I laid out in Chapter 2) that political justification is addressed. This justification succeeds when justificatory reasons could not be rejected by people conceived of in this way. In different parts of Rawls' work, we find different accounts of the beliefs to be attributed to ideal people which explain why they accept that pluralism is a permanent fact. In 'Justice as Fairness: Political not Metaphysical', the suggestion is that ideal people accept the permanence of pluralism in virtue of accepting that values are incommensurable. I argued that the philosophical controversiality of theses of incommensurability means that those seeking a minimally demanding approach to political justification should prefer an alternative account of why ideal people accept the permanence of pluralism, if there is one available.

A less demanding account is found in Rawls' *Political Liberalism*. Here, the claim is that ideal people accept the permanence of pluralism in virtue of accepting the burdens of judgement (which is why Rawls stresses, in that book, that pluralism is to be thought of as reasonable). This explanation does not require that people accept philosophical theses as controversial as the incommensurability view, but it does require that people conceive of their own judgement as burdened; that is, that they accept that, even in ideal conditions, they cannot expect to convince all others who disagree with them – even on the most trivial matters – of the error of their judgement. I claimed that this demand requires a uniformity of belief about the operation of judgement which it would be desirable to avoid, if possible.

My suggestion at the end of Chapter 2 was that we start by assuming that all people are motivationally committed to their self-respect, and that they accept that this is true of others with whom they share a constituency of justification. If self-respect can be developed and maintained in a multiplicity of ways, then assuming this motivational commitment makes pluralism (albeit not reasonable pluralism) a permanent fact. For this 'many flowers' view to compete with the incommensurability and burdens views required answers to two questions. (1) How does attributing a belief in this explanation of the permanence of pluralism affect the demandingness of justificatory reasons for a liberal Constructivism taking this approach? (2) Can a Constructivist procedure incorporating the many flowers view justify liberal principles of toleration and public reason? Chapters 2 and 3 addressed these questions.

In Chapter 2 I argued that self-respect is a matter of congruence according to a non-subservient self-conception. In making these arguments I attempted to show that an explanation of the permanence of pluralism in terms of the permanence of peoples' motivational commitments to their own self-respect does not require either of the following of stage 2 people. First, philosophically controversial judgements of the relative value of different sets of values: many different sets of values can meet the congruence and non-subservience requirements and so provide the grounds for self-respect. Second, philosophically controversial judgements about the equality of persons: non-subservience preserves a person's status as a reason-giving and receiving creature, and does not require that she conceive of herself as equal in value to all others. These two features of the account of self-respect mean that ideal people can be thought of as being motivationally committed to their own self-respect without having to acquire controversial beliefs about the superiority of some sets of values over others, or an egalitarian conception of human value. In this way the many flowers view is less demanding than the incommensurability view.

The many flowers view requires that ideal people are committed to their own self-respect and believe that all other people are committed to their self-respect. For the diversity in the constituency of justification that stage 2 people acknowledge to be accepted by them as permanent, these people have to accept that the self-respect of others may depend on values and activities very different from those to which their own self-respect responds. This might make it appear that the same problem of demandingness arises for the many flowers view as arises for the burdens view. In the same way that the burdens view asks that people revise their conception of what it means for their beliefs to be true, doesn't the many flowers view require that people revise their conception of what it means for them to be committed to their own self-respect?

It does not, because of a disanalogy between what we think of as involved in having a belief and what we think of as involved in being committed to one's self-respect. The many flowers view is less demanding than the burdens view because of the difference between what the operation of judgement aims at and what the motivational commitment to self-respect aims at. The burdens view requires that people accept the possibility that they could never convince any other person of any of their beliefs, even in ideal conditions. Because judgement aims at the acquisition of true beliefs, conceiving of judgement as standing under burdens has the uncomfortable consequence that those who accept the burdens of judgement, and believe that their beliefs are true, must also accept that even in ideal conditions they cannot be sure of convincing any others of these true beliefs. Although there is no formal contradiction in believing that one's belief that P is true and believing that one could never convince others who exercise their reason correctly to believe that P (the claim is not that the burdens view demands the epistemically impossible), it is nevertheless asking much of people that they believe both of these things with respect to all of their beliefs. Most of us, when we believe that a belief of ours is true, believe that we could convince others to share that belief, if only conditions were ideal: we treat the truth of any belief of ours as evidence that the correct exercise of reason by others would bring them to see the truth of this belief. To require that people relinquish this conception of what it means for them to have true beliefs is demanding. And the question of whether people are correct to hold this conception of belief or not is irrelevant: the aim of liberal political justification is not to inculcate true beliefs in people, but to generate justificatory reasons which persons could not reject, given a characterisation of them which keeps the constituency of justification as diverse as possible.

If there were no alternative to the burdens view then the demands it makes of people might be the least we can expect, and the limits to diversity it creates in any constituency of justification might be thought of as unavoidable. But my aim has been to sketch an alternative, less demanding picture of Constructivist liberal political justification which yields the same liberal results as Constructivism informed by the burdens view. The key to this picture is that ideal people at stage 2 of justification are committed to their own self-respect, and acknowledge that all others are too. This is less demanding than the burdens view because the consequences of being committed to the truth of one's beliefs and of being motivationally committed to one's own self-respect differ. Because self-respect does not aim at truth, we would not expect a person who is committed to their self-respect to believe that she can convert all others to her path to self-respect. Because self-respect does not aim at truth, a commitment to certain values as the basis of one's own self-respect does not entail a commitment to the belief that all others can be brought to share those values, in ideal conditions. Attributing to all ideal persons a commitment to their own self-respect, and a belief that all others similarly committed may not achieve self-respect in the same way, is less demanding than the burdens view, because there is no reason to think that the first commitment is in tension with the second belief, given the way we think about our own self-respect. We think that the truth of our beliefs somehow reaches out to the belief systems of others; but we don't believe that the grounds of our own self-respect should seep into the grounds others have for their self-respect. On the many flowers view, no radical revision is required in our conception of what it means to be committed to our own self-respect in order for this commitment to be consistent with accepting the permanence of pluralism.

The next step is to show that Constructivism informed by the many flowers view of pluralism yields liberal results: this has been the aim of this chapter. Tracing connections between self-respect and practical reason as it addresses questions of justice establishes that self-respect – whatever its bases in values and practices – is an idea of practical reason and so ought to be included as an aspect of stage 2 persons in any liberal Constructivism. The argument that a person's commitment to her own self-respect means that she could not reject reasons to endorse procedures of justification informed by public reason shows that making self-respect central to the stage 2 conception of the person is sufficient for the justification of liberal principles. And if we seek the least demanding account of justificatory reasons consistent with these reasons supporting liberal principles, then many flowers Constructivism is necessary for the justification of these principles too.

The book so far has just addressed questions about the procedure of liberal Constructivist justification, and how it is best conceived: there has been virtually no discussion of the consequences of conceiving of justification in this way for principles and institutions. In the final chapter I give a detailed account of the social bases of self-respect, and raise questions about the implications of reasons to promote and support the social bases of self-respect being non-rejectable by ideal persons. The next chapter gives an idea of the sorts of questions about principles of justice which are raised by a liberal Constructivism informed by the justificatory value of self-respect. In the chapter after that I conclude with a review of the argument of the book as a whole.

5
The Social Bases of Self-Respect

5.1 Introduction

The argument so far has been that self-respect provides a necessary and minimally demanding context for justice-oriented practical reasoning. Given that a person's self-respect and the conditions in which it is normally developed ensure – insofar as anything can – that the person will be committed to procedures of justification informed by public reason, liberal Constructivists can avoid Rawls' demanding requirement that membership of the constituency of justification requires acceptance of the burdens of judgement, as well as the even more demanding requirement that such membership depends on a belief in some philosophically controversial thesis of incommensurability.

Once we understand self-respect as providing the context for justice-oriented practical reasoning, the social bases of self-respect assume a fresh significance in political justification. If self-respect is of fundamental importance in political justification because it is necessary for strongly evaluative, justice-oriented practical reasoning, then the social bases of self-respect are of fundamental importance because the development of persons' self-respect will be severely impeded in the absence of these opportunities: persons' capacities to give and assess reasons in political justification will be deformed if the basic structure of their society inhibits the development of their self-respect. A liberal commitment to an inclusive constituency of justification entails a commitment to creating social conditions in which all persons have the opportunity to develop and maintain self-respect. On a self-respect based Constructivist approach, a commitment to the creation of these conditions is just part of what it is to be committed to the project of liberal political justification itself. This concluding chapter raises some questions about how to interpret principles of justice which aim at a fair distribution of the social bases of self-respect for all. This chapter does not answer these questions; rather, the point is to illustrate how a commitment to self-respect and its social bases as a core justificatory value can shape liberal thinking about the political justification of principles of equal liberty and economic justice.

Let me recap on what I have claimed about self-respect and its social contexts so far. A person's self-respect depends on her achieving congruence between her non-subservient self-conception and self-expression through some success according to individual criteria of excellence. The pursuit of success according to individual criteria normally takes place in communities of shared interests, wherein such success can be recognised as such and esteemed by others. This increases the self-respecting person's confidence that her individual criteria are worth pursuing, and that she is the kind of person who is fit to pursue them, which encourages her to continue to seek congruence. However, as the case of the Stepford Wives showed, congruence is sufficient for self-respect if and only if it is achieved against the background of a non-subservient self-conception, which reflects the fact that a self-respecting person sees herself as worthy of being given justifying reasons. The account of non-subservience given in Chapter 2 was cashed out in counterfactual terms: to establish whether a person is subservient we must consider whether she would judge to be legitimate her expectations of others that they give her justifying reasons for any demands they make of her. This makes it hard to determine whether any particular person is subservient; but given that we cannot look into one another's hearts, this is a virtue of the counterfactual account.

How does this account of self-respect translate into an account of its social bases? A good place to start is with Rawls, who gives the social bases of self-respect a prominent place on his list of primary goods. He states that:

> self-respect depends upon and is encouraged by certain public features of basic social institutions, how they work together and how people who accept these arrangements are expected to (and

normally do) regard and treat one another. These features of basic institutions and publicly expected (and normally honoured) ways of conduct are the social bases of self-respect.[1]

On my account, the social bases of self-respect are opportunities for the development of a non-subservient self-conception and the achievement of congruence through success according to individual criteria of excellence. The reason why self-respect enters justificatory arguments through considerations about its *social* bases is, quite simply, that self-respect is not a good which can be distributed to persons directly: self-respect is a matter of achievement of a certain sort, given a self-conception satisfying the counterfactual test for non-subservience. Neither of these aspects of self-respect can be secured directly for a person by political means: the most we can do is to provide persons with opportunity to develop these aspects of self-respect.

Although self-respect cannot be provided directly with political measures, political and social conditions can present severe obstacles to success according to individual criteria of excellence, and can systematically encourage subservience across whole swathes of persons. It is the avoidance of these conditions that political justification informed by the value of self-respect aims at, through assessment of whether various sets of social and political conditions count as social bases of self-respect. When assessing social and political conditions as social bases of self-respect we need to think about how they might assist or hinder people in the search for congruence through success according to individual criteria of excellence, and how they might encourage or obstruct the development of a non-subservient self-conception. Although it may be hard to tell from the outside whether any particular person is non-subservient – or, indeed, has genuinely achieved congruence – this does not prevent us from identifying certain social and political conditions as normally conducive or damaging to the development of self-respect, and this is what we need for considerations about the social bases of self-respect to be factored into political justifications.

In his general conception of justice, Rawls includes the social bases of self-respect in the scope of a maximin pattern of distribution.

All social primary goods – liberty and opportunity, income and wealth, and the social bases of self-respect – are to be distributed equally unless an unequal distribution of any, or all, of these values is to the advantage of the least favoured.[2]

However, when it comes to stating the special conception of justice in terms of principled, patterned distributions of the social primary goods, reference to the social bases of self-respect is absent. In the special conception of justice, the first principle distributes rights and liberties, and the second principle distributes economic goods and opportunities: there is no principle just dedicated to distribution of the social bases of self-respect.[3] The reason for this, as I indicated in Chapter 2, is that a maximin distribution of the social bases of self-respect is supposed to supervene on the distribution of the other primary goods secured by Rawls' two principles. This means that distributions of primary goods are to be assessed according to whether they are maximin when the good in question, and its pattern of distribution, is understood as a social basis of self-respect. So, when using a maximin distribution of the social bases of self-respect as a benchmark of the just distribution of a good, we must ask: (1) how, if at all, does the good itself provide individuals who have it with opportunity for self-respect?, and (2) how, if at all, does the pattern of the good's distribution create opportunity for self-respect for all those who receive the good according to this pattern? Answering the first question establishes whether the good itself is a means to self-respect for persons, whereas answering the second question establishes the range of permissible inequalities in the good understood as a social basis of self-respect. For Rawls, when liberties are equal and can be restricted only for the sake of other liberties; when opportunities are equal, and equalising opportunity takes priority over maximinning economic advantage; and when the distribution of income and wealth is maximin, consistent with the just savings principle, and takes priority over efficiency and maximising overall levels of welfare, then a maximin distribution of the social bases of self-respect is secured.

For the purposes of this chapter I shall simply uncritically adopt the maximin principle of distribution for goods laid out in Rawls' general conception of justice. Making this assumption allows for an assessment of various distributions of rights and liberties, opportunities, and income and wealth as securing a maximin distribution of the social bases of self-respect. A different general conception of justice specifying a different pattern of distribution – say, sufficiency or strict equality as opposed to maximin – will yield different conclusions about how distributions of specific goods contribute to or damage a just distribution of the social bases of self-respect. My reason for making this assumption is that we need some principle of distribution to work with when assessing how making the social bases of self-respect central to political justification would affect our thinking about questions of distribution, and maximin is a prominent and much discussed proposal. For those who reject maximin, the discussions of this chapter should nevertheless illustrate how the social bases of self-respect supervene on distributions of the other primary goods, thus opening the door to reflections about what a non-maximin distribution of the social bases of self-respect might demand with respect to specific distributions of the other primary goods.

5.2   Taxonomy

How are the social bases of self-respect manifested in specific distributions of the other primary goods? Here we must begin by identifying what counts as an opportunity for self-respect, and then consider how distributions of the other primary goods might realise a maximin distribution of these opportunities.[4]

One site of opportunity for self-respect is associational life, in two senses. First, associations can provide resources specific to them and necessary for associates' pursuit of their individual criteria of excellence. These resource/associational bases of self-respect are specific to particular communities of reciprocal esteem, and are not universally necessary for the pursuit of any self-respecting plan. For example, a person whose self-respect is focused on sporting achievement requires resources like equipment and training expertise found in associations dedicated to sport, or a person whose self-respect depends on political activism may need access to computers and software for desk top publishing political pamphlets and newsletters.

The second way in which associational life can provide a social basis of self-respect is through the mutual recognition between members. Mutual recognition in close associations of reciprocal esteem realises opportunity for self-respect because these associations are sites at which the companion effect to the Aristotelian principle can be experienced. When activity aiming at success according to individual criteria is recognised as successful by others, the self-conception to which these criteria are attached is confirmed, which makes continued congruence possible.

The associational bases of self-respect found in communities of shared interests provide resource and recognitional bases of self-respect. These communities are established and develop in response to the emergence and development of particular self-respect related interests among disparate individuals; the set of such communities sufficient as resource/associational or recognitional/associational bases of self-respect for all people existing at any one time will not necessarily be sufficient at another time. The networks of associations in which people find the social bases of their self-respect are in constant flux because the pursuit of success according to individual criteria of excellence governed by the Aristotelian principle means that what counts as self-respect supporting success for each individual changes over time. As the content of diverse individual criteria of excellence evolves, new associations form which are sensitive to the resource- and recognitional-needs of these evolved criteria, as a consequence of like-minded self-respecters seeking out one another in the pursuit of success according to their individual criteria.

Opportunity for self-respect requires access to these associations, and this access is provided via various distributions of 'framework resources', that is, resources distributed through the framework of the basic structure. On a Rawlsian account, the social primary goods of liberty, opportunity, and income and wealth are framework resources for self-respect: these goods provide access to diverse forms of associational life in which persons can pursue their self-respect in multifarious ways.

However, the significance of framework resources for self-respect is not exhausted by their instrumental role in providing access to the associational bases of self-respect. We have seen that self-respect is sensitive to the judgements of others in close associations, so that such associations provide recognitional bases of self-respect. A related significant feature of framework resources can be seen once we consider how, in addition to providing practical means to membership of diverse associations in which self-respect can be developed, the *pattern* of their distribution can also encourage or impede the development of self-respect. The self-respect related symbolism of patterns of distribution of framework resources is explained once we remember that self-respect is normally sensitive to the judgements of those with whom a person is in political community, as well as those with whom she is in close association. In discussion of the social bases of self-respect Rawls claims that:

> what is necessary is that there should be for each person at least one community of shared interests to which he belongs and where he finds his endeavours confirmed by his associates. *And for the most part this assurance is sufficient whenever in public life citizens respect one another's ends and adjudicate their political claims in ways that also support their self-esteem.*[5]

A person who finds her self-respect in associational membership and the activities that go with it normally also finds her self-respect supported when those with whom she is not closely associated, but with whom she shares citizenship, include her in public justificatory debate by offering her justificatory reasons in public reason, and by taking seriously the reasons she offers and sincerely takes to be presentable in public reason. This form of inclusion can serve as a further recognitional basis of self-respect.[6] The reason why this mutual recognition between citizens can constitute a social basis of self-respect is that self-respect depends on a person's conception of herself as worthy of being given justifying reasons by any other person capable of having expectations of her that she act in a certain way. The fact that a person is in a political community means that her fellow citizens will have expectations of her that she act in accordance with principles they decide upon in justificatory debate. When a person is excluded from such debate – either by having her reasons ignored or by not being offered reasons by others at all – her status as a person worthy of giving and receiving justificatory reasons is questioned, and the non-subservience upon which her self-respect depends is under threat.

This mutual recognition between citizens constitutes a further possible recognitional basis of self-respect, but one which is realised in the framework of society, as opposed to the byways of associational life. This basis of self-respect is also related to the distribution of framework resources, for the following reasons. In addition to how framework resources serve as practical means to self-respect, the pattern of their distribution counts as a recognitional basis of self-respect because it symbolises the relations between persons as citizens who share a political community within which these resources are to be distributed. For example, a distribution of the right to freedom of speech which excluded black people would count as an attack on their opportunity for self-respect not just because free speech is instrumental in gaining the benefits of associations of reciprocal esteem, but also because this restriction symbolises a conception of black people by non-blacks either as being incapable of offering reasons in justificatory debate, or as being unworthy of being listened to or addressed. The distribution of the right to free speech in this case partly counts as an attack on the opportunity for self-respect of black people because the pattern according to which the framework resource of the right to free speech is distributed symbolises a conception of black people as subservient.

When patterns with such symbolism are deeply entrenched in the history and culture of a constituency of justification they can achieve what they symbolically aim at by creating subservience among those they exclude. The damage to opportunity for self-respect caused by failures of mutual recognition at the level of citizenship can, of course, be mitigated by the reciprocal esteem created by mutual recognition in close associations. However, the fact that most people do not find the associational conditions of self-respect in their membership of just one closed group standing in united opposition to the ideal of shared citizenship means that the recognitional bases of self-respect, as found in the patterns of distribution of framework resources, remain significant as social bases of self-respect.

We now have a more detailed version of the basic taxonomy of the social bases of self-respect given in Chapter 3.

Resource/associational bases of self-respect are the resources available within communities of reciprocal esteem which support self-respect. Access to these resources is secured by framework resources.

Recognitional/associational bases of self-respect are found in communities of reciprocal esteem wherein members experience the companion effect to the Aristotelian principle. Access to these communities is secured by framework resources.

Recognitional/framework bases of self-respect are found in the mutual recognition between citizens as participants in justificatory debate who view one another as capable and worthy of giving and receiving justificatory reasons. These bases are secured through the pattern of distribution of framework resources.

Resource/framework bases of self-respect are the resources available within the framework of the basic structure of society which serve as practical means to self-respect, either by providing access to the associational bases of self-respect, or in virtue of the symbolism of their pattern of distribution. These resources are distributed directly by principles of justice.

In sum, the opportunities for self-respect that matter from the point of view of justice are realised in the distribution of framework resources providing access to close associations in which activities oriented towards the satisfaction of individual criteria of excellence are normally pursued, and in which the companion effect to the Aristotelian principle can be experienced as a result of such pursuit. Opportunities for self-respect are also secured in the patterns of distribution of framework resources throughout the basic structure, which symbolise persons' attitudes towards one another as joint participants in the project of political justification.

Securing the associational bases of self-respect in their resource and framework aspects, and the recognitional aspect of the framework bases of self-respect, is a matter of determining what counts as a framework resource for self-respect, and the pattern according to which that resource should be distributed. In the next section (5.3) I review some arguments for equal liberty as a social basis of self-respect. In the final section (5.4) I identify three ways in which income and wealth can serve as a resource basis for self-respect, and I consider how economic inequalities might be thought of as damaging a maximin distribution of the social bases of self-respect. As I mentioned earlier, my aim is just to show what sorts of questions arise once we take self-respect and its social bases seriously as justificatory values, rather than to provide answers to the questions I raise. The point of the next two sections is to set an agenda for research for liberal Constructivists who accept the arguments of earlier chapters.

5.3   Framework resources I: equal liberty

How should basic liberties be distributed so as to maximin the social bases of self-respect? I shall make some general remarks about an equal distribution of basic rights and liberties as such a maximin distribution before raising some more specific questions about how freedom of association ought to be distributed so as to contribute to a maximin distribution of the social bases of self-respect, given the dynamics of group membership as a condition of self-respect.

In line with the taxonomy given in the last section, we need to assess how basic liberties serve as resources for enjoyment of the associational bases of self-respect, and how the pattern according to which these liberties are distributed serves as a recognitional basis of self-respect. The first sense in which liberty serves as a basis of self-respect is obvious: without liberty, a person will be unable to form and participate in communities of shared interests normally providing the associational bases of self-respect.[7] This general truth raises the important question of which particular liberties serve as framework/resource bases of self-respect. It seems clear enough here that the standard quadruplet of liberal freedoms are framework/resource bases of self-respect: freedom of movement, freedom of association, freedom of thought and freedom of expression. Without each of these freedoms a person will not be in a position to seek out and participate in associations of reciprocal esteem. This is particularly true once we recognise that most people do not remain within the communities of reciprocal esteem into which they are born or socialised, and many people's self-respect related projects continue to change and develop over their lives, necessitating movement from one group to another.

Turning to a consideration of liberty as a framework/recognitional basis of self-respect, we have to ask what pattern of the distribution of liberty maximins opportunity for self-respect. To be specific, we want to know whether an unequal distribution of liberty could make the worst off in this distribution as well off as possible in terms of how they are recognised by their fellow citizens as capable and worthy of participation in justificatory debate. The answer to this question has seemed fairly clear, at least to liberals: anything less than an equal distribution of liberty will undermine citizens' recognition of one another as capable and worthy participants in the project of political justification which they all unavoidably face together. For example, Rawls states that when liberty is equal:

> everyone has a similar and secure status when they meet to conduct the common affairs of the wider society. No one is inclined

to look beyond the constitutional affirmation of equality for further political ways of assuring his status. Nor, on the other hand, are men disposed to accept a lesser than equal liberty...[This would have] the effect of publicly establishing their inferiority as defined by the basic structure of society. This subordinate ranking in the public forum experienced in the attempt to take part in political and economic life, and felt in dealing with those who have a greater liberty, would indeed be humiliating and destructive of self-esteem.[8]

The quadruplet of standard liberal liberties secures access to the associational bases of self-respect, and enjoyment of the benefits of reciprocal esteem once membership has been achieved. Once these liberties are equalised they also serve as framework/recognitional bases of self-respect, and thus discourage subservience, at least in the political arena. *Prima facie*, a principle of liberty secures a maximin distribution of the social bases of self-respect if and only if it includes the standard liberal liberties, and keeps them equal.

This general conclusion about the distribution of liberty understood as a social basis of self-respect is *prima facie* because there are philosophical problems with respect to how the exercise of liberty by one person or group in the pursuit of their self-respect may damage the exercise of that same liberty by another person or group in *their* pursuit of their self-respect. For example, there are heated debates in the literature about whether a pornographer's freedom of expression *qua* resource/framework basis of self-respect for him undermines freedom of expression *qua* social basis of self-respect for women. When a good seems to serve as a social basis of self-respect for one person or group only when it is denied to another person or group in pursuit of their self-respect then we have to consider whether a pattern of inequality in that particular liberty is maximin with respect to the good understood as a recognitional framework basis of self-respect; that is, we have to consider whether the presumption in favour of equality with respect to that good is more than *prima facie*. Much has been written on freedom of expression and censorship as they relate to opportunity for self-respect.[9] However, much less has been written on the idea of freedom of association as a social basis of self-respect, where similar questions arise.[10]

What particular freedoms should be understood as contributing to freedom of association as a resource basis of self-respect? Clearly, the right of exit from groups is fundamental to freedom of association so understood. Forcing a person to stay in a group can seriously damage her self-respect. Such coercion can prevent her from engaging in activities not indexed to those of the group which may provide her with new and more exciting materials to serve as the focus of her self-respect. Of course, coercion can take many different forms, and each type of coercion requires a different exit-protecting right. For example, depriving people of the information necessary for them to know that exit is a legal option for them constitutes a form of coercion damaging to opportunity for self-respect. Hence, we need some form of civic education programme to ensure that such knowledge is imparted, particularly to the young.[11] Furthermore, a lack of economic means may impede exit, and so principles of distributive justice will be relevant here. The hope is that people will not have to insist upon their rights or call upon the coercive force of the state to aid their exit, but this cannot be assumed.

However, individual exit rights are not sufficient to secure exit in a way that is meaningful for self-respect. Exit from a group will lack such meaning if there are no other groups providing the associational bases of self-respect. Freedom to exit a group has significance as a resource basis of self-respect only if society as a whole contains a rich and diverse variety of groups providing the associational bases of self-respect. Such diversity is, and for the same reasons, a condition of opportunity for self-respect for those who, rather than voluntarily leaving their groups, are either forcibly excluded from groups, or prevented from making initial entry into them by members exercising their right to freedom of association via the application of exclusion rules. Exclusion or forcible ejection is damaging to opportunity for self-respect, first, if the ejected or excluded member's self-respect is premised on activities and standards peculiar to the group which rejects her; and second, if there exist no other suitable groups willing to accept her as a member. So there are two reasons why a diversity of groups in society constitutes a resource basis of self-respect. First, even if no movement between groups is necessary for self-respect, everyone is different and so needs membership of a different group to gain access to associational bases of self-respect suitable for them. And second, when movement across groups is necessary for self-respect, there has to exist a diversity of such groups for movement to be possible.

It is in the light of these reflections that some liberals have argued that maximin opportunity for self-respect requires special, 'multiculturalist' measures to protect, even encourage, diversity in society.[12] Multiculturalist measures to protect groups transcend both toleration *qua* non-interference, and non-discrimination policies which grant access to important political, social and economic institutions. Multiculturalist principles aim, beyond this, to grant protection to cultural groups providing associational bases of self-respect for their members, and resource conditions of self-respect for all in virtue of their multiplicity. Such measures might include language rights, exemptions from health and safety regulations attaching to certain forms of employment, public recognition of religious feast days and festivals, or the right to educate children in a particular culture.[13]

Another aspect of freedom of association which makes it plausible as a resource basis for self-respect is that it entails the right to exclude.[14] The right to adopt exclusionary membership policies *prima facie* serves as a resource basis of self-respect: a group may need to exclude outsiders to preserve its character as an associational basis of self-respect. A group which provides a forum in which, for example, talents for creative writing can be honed or in which soccer skills can be exercised in pursuit of a Sunday league cup endangers this provision if it admits to membership barely literate people or people physically unable to acquire soccer skills. The exclusion rules of many groups express criteria for membership which are necessary for the group to preserve its status as a site of opportunity for self-respect for its members, and for people with talents and abilities similar to its members.

Exclusion rules often preserve a group's status as a social basis of self-respect for those with shared interests and talents sufficient for them to meet criteria of membership. But a problem arises with respect to a person who shares the interests of group members but who lacks their level of talent, and for whom no other group will provide association fit to support her self-respect. The problem here is that to provide the untalented person with the associational bases of self-respect would require interfering with the exclusion rules of the group she aims to enter; but in so doing the status of that group as an associational basis of self-respect for extant and prospective talented members is diminished, or perhaps destroyed.

There are two broad types of response we might make here, both of which turn on what is involved in maximinning freedom of association *qua* social basis of self-respect. First, if interference with the exclusion rule in question would only diminish, not destroy, the group as a social basis of self-respect for extant and prospective talented members, and would provide the untalented prospective member with the opportunity for self-respect which she would otherwise lack, then maximin with respect to the social bases of self-respect demands that we interfere. Maximin requires that we aim to make the worst off person as well off as possible, even when this requires making the best off worse off. In this case the best off are talented extant and prospective members of the exclusionary group, and it is acceptable – so the response would go – that they be made worse off in terms of their opportunity for self-respect if this increases this opportunity for those with little or none of it.

The second response is that if interference with the exclusion rule would destroy the group as a site of opportunity for self-respect for talented extant and prospective members, then interference with the rule to increase the opportunity for self-respect of an untalented prospective member may not be justified. This would be the case if those who lose the group as a site of opportunity for self-respect as a result of state interference with its exclusion rules are left in a worse position than the position of the erstwhile worst off whose opportunity for self-respect is increased by interference with the rule. If this is the case, the distribution of freedom of association *qua* social basis of self-respect is not maximin because the worst off under the new distribution created by interference with the exclusion rule are worse off than the worst off under a distribution in which the rule is not interfered with.

Another set of considerations relates to the content of the exclusion rule in question. Some exclusion rules express criteria which are clearly and straightforwardly relevant to participation in the activities around which the group with the rule revolves. For example, the requirement that a person be able to play the bugle properly in order to join a marching band, the requirement that a person have reached a high level of physical fitness in order to join the army, or the requirement that a person have no record of child abuse in order to become a teacher or youth worker. But the relevance of many other rules to the activities of the group who apply them are either deeply dubious or highly contested. As an example of the first category, think of the historical exclusion of women from institutions of higher education on the grounds of their natural unsuitability for learning, or the exclusion of 'out' homosexuals from the US Army. As an example of the second category, think of the requirement that men entering the Catholic priesthood take a vow of chastity (or, indeed, the requirement that they be men), or the exclusion of women from various men's social clubs in London, such as the Garrett club.

These two sets of considerations – about the consequences of interference with exclusion rules, and the legitimacy of the rules themselves – must guide liberal thinking about the distribution of freedom of association as a social basis of self-respect. But we should form our judgements along both dimensions with extreme caution, since questions about how to identify the purposes of a group, so as to judge the legitimacy of its exclusion rules and the effect of interference with them, will be very hard to make from the outside. A healthy scepticism is called for with respect to the possibility of accurately classifying groups and correctly assessing the relevance and significance of existing exclusion rules to this classification. This is especially so given that the forcible introduction of new members to a group previously concerned to keep them out is likely to encounter resistance among extant members, and perhaps temporarily disrupt the group's pursuit of its purposes, whatever they are.

Nevertheless, such judgements must be made if we are to think about maximinning the social bases of self-respect through the distribution of freedom of association. Aside from the arguments I have given in this book for thinking that this is a good idea, I think we have intuitions about how such judgements must go, and indeed we have some legal precedents. The United States Supreme Court forced the Jaycees to admit women as full members.[15] Should the reasoning in this decision lead us to recommend that the Welsh Male Voice Choir admit women? If not, what is the difference between the Jaycees and the Welsh Male Voice Choir? If we think, as many liberals do, that the exclusion of out homosexuals from the US Army is illegitimate, then do similar self-respect related considerations apply to the exclusion of heterosexuals by gay groups? If we are opposed to exclusion in the first case, does that mean we are committed to banning gay-only night clubs? Again, assuming that we generally favour historically black educational establishments like Howard University, are we thereby also committed to giving support to organisations like the Nation of Islam? By assessing the extent to which groups such as these serve as social bases of self-respect in virtue of the exclusion rules they employ, we can start to think about the differences between them, and make cautious judgements about whether maximin with respect to the social bases of self-respect requires interference with their policies of exclusion.

5.4   Framework resources II: income and wealth

How does the distribution of income and wealth contribute to a maximin distribution of the social bases of self-respect? To answer this question we need to consider the senses in which the framework resource of income and wealth serves as a social basis of self-respect. As with liberty, we assess this resource as a social basis of self-respect by considering (1) whether and how it provides access to the associational bases of self-respect wherein community-specific resource and recognitional bases of self-respect are found, and (2) whether and how the pattern of its distribution symbolises membership of an inclusive constituency of justification. Let me consider how income and wealth serves as a framework resource for self-respect in each of these ways, starting with how it provides access to the associational bases of self-respect.

There are three ways in which income and wealth can serve as a resource basis of self-respect by providing opportunity for self-respect.

1. Income and wealth gives a person freedom to change jobs (or, if she has enough of it, to be free from work altogether) for the sake of her self-respect (the 'freedom-benefit'). Income and wealth brings this benefit because work place communities do not always provide people with the associational bases of self-respect, and sometimes directly damage a person's self-respect by demanding activities in direct conflict with the values informing her self-respect.
2. Income and wealth affects the quantity of leisure-time available to those in paid employment, where leisure-time is often where associational life is lived (the 'leisure-quantity' benefit). This benefit of income and wealth is important both for people whose work directly damages their self-respect, and for people whose work provides only partial support for their self-respect, and who need to look beyond the horizons of the work place for associational support for their self-respect.

3. Income and wealth affects the quality of leisure time available (the 'leisure-quality benefit'). Associational life as it supports self-respect – whether it is found inside or outside the work place – creates costs for participants who want to participate fully, even if these are only incidental costs associated with proper participation in the social life of the group.

Income and wealth brings opportunity for self-respect in virtue of the freedom and time it can buy, and how it can serve as an all purpose means granting access to associational life. Thinking about how the distribution of income and wealth might contribute to a maximin distribution of the social bases of self-respect just as a resource basis, then, requires us to think about how make the worst off people in terms of the freedom, leisure-quantity, and leisure-quality benefits of income and wealth as well off as possible. Who are these worst off people?

The worst off in this sense are people in paid employment which causes direct damage to their self-respect, leaves them no time to pursue self-respect related projects in associational life outside of work, and pays them so little that – even if they had the time – they could not afford to participate in the communities wherein rewarding associational lives can be led. I take it that many people in our society in low paid, menial, exhausting work – whether this is a full-time job with long hours or several part-time jobs with no fringe benefits – are in this position. The question is how income and wealth could be distributed so as to make these people better off in terms of the three benefits listed above.

One suggestion worth pursuing is that this maximin distribution can be achieved through unconditional basic income (UBI). The idea behind UBI is simple. Under a UBI scheme each person receives a grant fixed at the highest sustainable level regardless of their past, present or future work contribution, their willingness to work and their income from any other source.[16] This could promote maximin with respect to the three self-respect related benefits of income and wealth in the following ways.

1. UBI would increase the freedom benefit of income and wealth for those worst off in terms of it. Ideally, UBI would be set at above subsistence level, which would mean that no person would be

forced to take a job directly damaging to her self-respect. UBI would give unlucky people who do not find the associational bases of self-respect in the work place a degree of bargaining power with respect to their employers, actual and potential: either improve the quality of employment, or labour will be withheld.

2. The freedom benefit UBI brings would also improve the position of those worst off in terms of the leisure-quantity benefit. Again, if UBI is set at above subsistence level, such people can demand reasonable hours and holidays from employers, and withdraw their labour if the employer refuses.

3. Finally, UBI set at above subsistence level would improve the position of the worst off in terms of the quality of their associational life. Participation in most groups providing the associational bases of self-respect will not be financially costless. Even if it is just a matter of covering incidental costs associated with travel and the social activities which attach to most memberships, the quality of associational life can be damaged if a person lacks any funds beyond what are required to keep her alive. UBI would give those who lack these funds an extra source of income which could be used to improve the quality of their associational life.

Of course, each of these arguments needs to be made in far more depth, and no arguments for UBI are without practical and theoretical challenges.[17] On the practical side, some people worry that, rather than empowering workers in terms of the freedom benefit, UBI would operate as a subsidy to employers paying low wages. Another worry is that UBI would destroy incentives, and is unsustainable for that reason. The tax rates necessary to sustain UBI would be set so high, the objection goes, that most people would prefer not to work, which would then erode the tax base, making UBI impossible to sustain. Although these are tough objections, they are not insurmountable, and there is no consensus among economists that UBI could not work for these, or other, practical reasons.[18]

On the other side there are theoretical objections to UBI which must be overcome if discussion of the practical objections to it are ever to have significance. The greatest of these is the reciprocity objection. Crudely, this objection is that, not only is UBI an invitation to work shy and unscrupulous people to scrounge off hard working tax payers, but furthermore – and more seriously – UBI provides no grounds for criticism of scroungers. A more sophisticated state-ment of the reciprocity objection is given by Stuart White via his principle of 'baseline reciprocity'.

> Each person is entitled to a share of the economic benefits of social co-operation conferring equal opportunity (or real freedom) in return for the performance of an equal handicap-weighted quantum of contributive activity (hours of socially useful work, let us say, weighted by labour intensity).[19]

White's baseline reciprocity principle militates against UBI because UBI 'completely [detaches] the receipt of a decent minimum of the economic benefits of social co-operation from the satisfaction of a suitably defined reasonable work expectation'.[20]

At the heart of reciprocity objections to UBI is the idea that those who choose not to work ought not to impose the costs of that choice on others who choose to work, and thereby pay taxes. The thought is that justice in the distribution of economic goods is not done unless that distribution ensures that those who have made expensive choices – in this case, a choice of leisure over work – are held respon-sible for the costs of these choices, and UBI violates this condition by being unconditional. It is important to note that self-respect based arguments do not escape the reciprocity objection just in virtue of appealing to the self-respect related advantages of UBI: unless we claim that the personal bases of self-respect are beyond a person's control – which starts to make the search for self-respect look patho-logical – we must admit that a person has some responsibility for the way in which her self-respect develops.

The idea that distributive justice must reflect ideals of personal responsibility has dominated the literature on egalitarianism for at least the last fifteen years. However, it is not clear that this literature contains any workable account of what personal responsibility is, let alone of how we can apply such an account in our judgements of real life cases.[21] But beyond this problem, there are stirrings in the litera-ture which indicate a reaction against the idea that those committed to equality should have given away so much ground by making the ideal of personal responsibility so central to assessments of distribu-tive justice.[22] At the very least, a self-respect based argument for UBI reveals that the ideal of personal responsibility is in conflict with other cherished liberal values, and should make liberal egalitarians either clarify exactly what they are committed to via commitment to this ideal, or question whether they ought to be so committed, given what is lost once personal responsibility rules the day.[23]

Beyond considerations about how income and wealth serves as a resource basis of self-respect, we can also think about how the pattern of its distribution serves as a recognitional basis of self-respect. The suggested arguments for UBI are so far consistent with the idea that a very unequal distribution of income and wealth is a maximin distribution of the social bases of self-respect. There is so far no reason to think that making the worst off in terms of the self-respect related benefits of income and wealth *qua* framework resource as well off as possible requires making everyone equal in terms of the income and wealth which provides these benefits. The focus so far has been just on how income and wealth secures access to associational life in different ways; we have not yet considered how patterns of distribution of income and wealth might serve as recognitional framework bases of self-respect. If it can be shown that, even when large income and wealth inequalities are maximin from the point of view of income and wealth *qua* means to the associational bases of self-respect, the *symbolism* of extreme income and wealth inequalities damages the recognitional bases of self-respect for those worst off in these distributions, then it will have been shown that maximin with respect to income and wealth *qua* social basis of self-respect – understood in the fullest sense – places limits on permissible inequalities which are absent when income and wealth is considered only as a means to the associational bases of self-respect.

How might we think about the self-respect related symbolism of economic inequality? Here, we might invoke the idea of 'socially-located' egalitarianism, as described by Richard Norman.[24] Here, equality matters,

> not as a *means* to certain kinds of social relations, but as a way of *characterising* certain kinds of social relations. We might say that a society in which the power to make decisions about the society's common activities, and the benefits and burdens of social co-operation, are distributed as equally as possible will be, to that extent, a society in which desirable kinds of relations obtain between members.[25]

Socially-located egalitarianism means that a non-Pareto optimal but more or less equal distribution of income and wealth might be more justified than a Pareto-optimal but very unequal distribution, if the Pareto-optimal distribution damages desirable relations between members of political society.[26] Given a socially-located approach to the distribution of income and wealth, and taking maximin opportunity for self-respect as the key to desirable relations between members, we need to ask how much inequality in the distribution of income and wealth is consistent with preserving these desirable relations.

The relations that hold between members of political society serve as recognitional opportunities for self-respect when they permit active participation in justificatory debate governed by public reason.[27] In that case, we should start by thinking about which characteristics encourage persons to view one another as capable and worthy of an exchange of justificatory reasons, and how economic inequality might encourage the best off to view the worst off as lacking these characteristics, or indeed, encourage the worst off to view themselves as lacking these characteristics. If political society serves as a recognitional basis of self-respect at all, it does so by encouraging social relations wherein each person views all the others as capable of and entitled to engage in justificatory debate through the use of public reason. Unless each person views all others in this way, some people will be viewed by their fellow citizens as unworthy of being given justifying reasons, which can encourage subservience. If the pattern of income and wealth distribution as a social basis of self-respect places limits on permissible income and wealth inequalities, then it must be argued that some inequalities and not others damage mutual recognition between citizens in political society, who view one another as capable of giving justificatory reasons, worthy of having these reasons listened to, and worthy of being given reasons in return.

We could argue as follows. In a market economy, economic success is commonly taken to be an indicator of hard work, initiative and talent. Conversely, economic failure is often taken to indicate laziness, dependency and a lack of talent. With attitudes like these rife among the economically advantaged, the danger is that the economically disadvantaged come to share this view of themselves, and subservience spreads among them as they start to think that it is illegitimate for lazy, stupid and dependent people like themselves to have expectations that hard working, talented and independent people like the best off should offer them justifying reasons for whatever demands they make of them. When a political society is divided in the minds of some, or all, citizens into a class of people who deserve to be included in justificatory debate and a class of people who deserve to be excluded, it does not provide a maximin distribution of the framework/recognitional bases of self-respect. Were those who see their society as divided in this way to lose this belief, those who they now see as unworthy of partnership in justificatory debate (themselves, perhaps) would gain an opportunity for self-respect through this recognition without anyone else losing such an opportunity. This consequence of inequality is undesirable from the point of view of what David Miller calls the ideal of 'social equality': 'In objecting to inequality, we are objecting to social relations that we find unseemly – they involve incomprehension and mistrust between rich and poor, for instance, or arrogance on one side and forelock-tugging on the other'.[28]

Of course, it is very often the case that success and failure in market economies has absolutely nothing to do with the possession or lack of these characteristics, and everything to do with brute luck in the form of inherited privilege of one form or another, or unearned talents. And here an objection the argument just laid out will arise. Rather than arguing for a limit to the inequalities which encourage people to view one another as unworthy of being given justifying reasons, why not argue instead that these beliefs are false, and that people ought to shed them? In that case, no redistribution to limit economic inequality is necessary, because even large inequalities would be no barrier to political society serving as a framework/recognitional basis of self-respect.

Assessing the success of this objection takes us into difficult territory related to the question of what attitudes and beliefs ought to be taken as given among real people to whom political justification is ultimately to be addressed. I have argued in this book that we ought to aim for a minimally demanding version of liberal Constructivism which nevertheless yields justificatory reasons with critical power. I have argued that conceiving of stage 2 persons as caring about their self-respect and its social conditions is minimally demanding, and yields critically potent reasons through the commitment to public reason that a person's self-respect carries. However, beyond this it might be argued that there are realities about the way in which people and groups relate to one another in the world which mean that further beliefs not related to their self-respect must be taken as given when constructing political justifications. The more we take as given in this way, the greater the likelihood that political justifications will be accepted, but the greater the danger that the reasons constituting these justifications will be critically weak, and instead just reflect the beliefs that people already have. But if we are to construct justifications with the ultimate aim of using them to convince real people then, without relinquishing the critical potency we build in by characterising stage 2 people in a certain way, we have to have an understanding of what we can and cannot expect people to change in terms of their beliefs, desires, and perceptions of one another. As we have just seen in the case of patterns of economic inequality, how we answer such questions can have a big effect on what we recommend in practice. At this point, we must look for help from historians, sociologists, and anthropologists: we cannot get answers to these questions within the limits of philosophy alone. However if, as I suspect, the negative judgements prompted by economic inequality are likely to be hard to uproot, then – at least for the time being – a self-respect based argument for limiting economic inequality should resonate with liberals who aim at creating inclusive constituencies of justification.

This concludes my discussion of the consequences of thinking about the distribution of the social bases of self-respect as supervenient on the distribution of the other primary goods from the point of view of maximin. Although the discussion has only touched the tip of the iceberg on this subject, I believe it shows the radical potential with respect to political principles of any liberal justification which includes self-respect and its social bases as central justificatory values. This, I take it, is a virtue of the account. Historically, liberal approaches were seen as presenting radical and exciting alternatives to dominant political practice, and this reputation was deserved. I think that the best forms of liberalism retain this radical potential, and that it is important to make this explicit.

Concluding Review

By way of conclusion, let me review the different stages of the argument presented in the last five chapters.

In Chapter 1 I laid out what I take to be a liberal conception of political justification in terms of the inclusiveness of the constituency of justification, and the permanence of deep diversity in that constituency. Once we understand justificatory reasons as practical reasons, as I claimed that we must, then questions about the motivational adequacy of these reasons arise. If justificatory reasons are supposed to be action-guiding then we have to ask two questions about them. (1) Is action for these reasons possible? The answer to this question is no if such action would require that members of the constituency of justification have contradictory beliefs or inconsistent motives. (2) How demanding are these justificatory reasons? The demandingness of a set of reasons is a function not of the formal possibility of action guided by them, but rather of the degree of uniformity along various dimensions required across a constituency of persons in order for them all to have the motivational commitment to act for these reasons. If a reason is motivationally adequate for a person if and only if she has a present motivational commitment to act for that reason (the 'sub-Humean' view of motivational adequacy), then questions of demandingness do not arise. Other conceptions according to which practical reasons are claimed to be motivationally adequate – externalism and deliberative internalism – face questions of demandingness.

With these preliminaries in place, I laid out the structure of Constructivist political justification in Chapter 2 using ideas from Rawls. I argued there that Rawls' own explanations as to why the ideal persons to whom justificatory reasons are addressed accept the permanence of pluralism make his justificatory reasons too demanding. If persons are only unable to reject reasons to practice toleration and endorse public reason once they accept theses of incommensurability, or radically revise their beliefs about what it means for them to have what they take to be true beliefs, then the diversity characteristic of liberal constituencies of justification is restricted. It might be thought that this is the best we can do; however, I suggested that by conceiving of ideal persons as committed to their own self-respect and its social conditions, and as accepting that all other people are likewise committed, we might find a less demanding set of reasons for endorsing public reason.

Consequently, in Chapters 3 and 4 I gave an account of self-respect and its social conditions which shows why people who are committed to their own self-respect, and who accept that all others are likewise committed, could not reject reasons to endorse public reason. The key points here were (1) that no restrictions were placed on the nature of self-respect apart from the congruence and non-subservience requirements, and (2) that asking a person to accept that the self-respect of others need not depend on their sharing the same values and participating in the same practices as she does does not require a radical revision of the way people think about their own self-respect. (1) means that a liberal constituency populated by self-respecting people can be thought of as deeply diverse. (2) means that this form of Constructivism is less demanding than Rawls' form, because reasons to endorse public reason do not become non-rejectable only when people are conceived of as having radically revised certain of their beliefs.

Chapter 5 has suggested ways in which treating the social bases of self-respect can affect the justification of principles distributing liberties and economic goods. By making the social bases of self-respect a central value in political justification, fresh perspectives on these questions can be gained. With respect to questions of liberty and group membership, a conception of groups as providers of opportunity for self-respect allows for a more fine-grained distinction between different sorts of groups which might support an unequal distribution of rights to freedom of association consistent with maximin: rights of exit must always be kept equal, but exclusion rules preventing entry may sometimes be permitted. And with respect to distributive justice, understanding income and wealth, and the pattern of its distribution, as social bases of self-respect should prompt liberals to think harder about the ideals informing the welfare state.

To sum up, the hackneyed criticism endlessly levelled against liberal principles of justice is that these principles are acceptable only to people who are already committed to secular liberal values of autonomy, individuality, progress, and independence. My aim in this book has been to present a version of liberal political justification which escapes this criticism in virtue of its Constructivist account of the right principles as principles which could not be rejected by people reasoning practically to address problems of justice, and in virtue of its characterisation of justice-oriented practical reasoning as intimately connected with the self-respect of the reasoner. If the arguments in this book are at all convincing then subtle worries about liberalism and pluralism have been assuaged, and the hackneyed criticisms of liberalism which amplify these worries can be put to rest.

Notes

Preface and Acknowledgements

1. For the most well-known version of this criticism see Michael Sandel, *Liberalism and the Limits of Justice* (Cambridge: Cambridge University Press, 1982).
2. The latest liberal attack on anti-liberal multiculturalism is Brian Barry, *Culture and Equality* (Cambridge: Polity Press, 2001).
3. This line of criticism takes its inspiration from Carol Gilligan, *In A Different Voice: Psychological Theory and Women's Moral Development* (Cambridge, Mass.: Harvard University Press, 1982).
4. See, for example, Richard Rorty, 'Postmodernist Bourgeois Liberalism', *Objectivity, Relativism and Truth* (Cambridge: Cambridge University Press, 1991), pp. 197–202.
5. John Rawls, *A Theory of Justice* (Oxford: Oxford University Press, 1971).

1 Introduction: The Practice of Political Justification

1. One notable recent exception to this claim is Christopher Bertram, 'Political Justification, Theoretical Complexity, and Democratic Community', *Ethics*, **107** (1997) 563–83. Bertram argues that those committed to the Enlightenment ideal of 'status egalitarianism' (p. 566) must aim for transparency as a mark of legitimacy in the ideal polity. This enables:

   the reconciliation of each person to the social order, either by supplying reasons why that order is legitimate or by proposing such adjustments as would make it acceptable to reasonable persons. (p. 565)

   Taking the ideal of transparency seriously requires political justifications which sincere non-specialist advocates could successfully communicate to sincere non-specialist recipients (p. 575). Bertram argues that such communication is only possible below a certain threshold of theoretical complexity.
2. A distribution of goods is Pareto-efficient when no one could be made better off in that distribution without someone else being made worse off.
3. For discussion of 'defeater' reasons see Gerald F. Gaus, *Justificatory Liberalism: An Essay on Epistemology and Political Theory* (New York: Oxford University Press, 1996), p. 144.
4. See Susan Mendus, *Impartiality in Moral and Political Philosophy* (Oxford: Oxford University Press, 2002) for a sensitive discussion of these issues.

5. See John Rawls, 'Reply to Habermas', *The Journal of Philosophy*, **XCII**(3) (March 1995), 132–80, esp. p. 175 ff.

6. A good example of such a cosmopolitan critique of Richard Rorty's approach to the question of scope is Norman Geras, *Solidarity in the Conversation of Humankind: The Ungroundable Liberalism of Richard Rorty* (London: Verso, 1995).

7. On the cosmopolitan side see, for example, Onora O'Neill, *Bounds of Justice* (Cambridge: Cambridge University Press, 2000); Charles Jones, *Global Justice: Defending Cosmopolitanism* (Oxford: Oxford University Press, 1999). On the non-cosmopolitan side see, for example, David Miller, *On Nationality* (Oxford: Oxford University Press, 1997).

8. Jeremy Waldron, 'Theoretical Foundations of Liberalism', *Philosophical Quarterly*, **37**(147) (1987), 127–50, p. 149. See also Jean Hampton 'The Common Faith Of Liberalism', *Pacific Philosophical Quarterly*, **75** (1994), 187–216.

9. John Rawls, *Political Liberalism* (New York: Columbia University Press, 1993), pp. 56–7.

10. Brian Barry, *Justice As Impartiality* (Oxford: Clarendon Press, 1995), p. 184. In chapter 7 Barry claims that Thomas Nagel, Charles Larmore, and John Rawls are all committed to his form of scepticism with respect to the views constitutive of deep diversity.

11. Brian Barry, *Justice As Impartiality*, p. 179. For assessment of this argument see Matt Matravers and Susan Mendus, 'The Reasonableness of Pluralism', Catriona McKinnon and Dario Castiglione (eds), *The Culture of Toleration in Diverse Societies: Reasonable Tolerance* (Manchester: Manchester University Press, 2002).

12. John Rawls, *Political Liberalism*, p. 63

13. Brian Barry, 'How Not to Defend Liberal Institutions', *Liberty and Justice: Essays in Political Theory II* (Oxford: Clarendon Press, 1991), p. 34.

14. Brian Barry, 'How Not to Defend Liberal Institutions', p. 38.

15. See Isaiah Berlin, 'The Pursuit of the Ideal' and 'The Decline of Utopian Ideas in the West', *The Crooked Timber of Humanity* (London: Fontana Press, 1990); 'Two Concepts of Liberty', *Four Essays on Liberty* (Oxford: Oxford University Press, 1969). See also Joseph Raz, *The Morality of Freedom* (Oxford: Clarendon Press, 1986); 'Incommensurability and Agency', *Incommensurability, Incomparability and Practical Reason*, Ruth Chang (ed.), (Cambridge, Mass.: Harvard University Press, 1997).

16. For an analysis of incommensurability based arguments for liberal toleration, see my 'Tolerance and the Character of Pluralism', *The Culture of Toleration in Diverse Societies: Reasonable Tolerance*, Catriona McKinnon and Dario Castiglione (eds).

17. Will Kymlicka, *Liberalism, Community and Culture* (Oxford: Clarendon Press, 1989).

18. See, for example, the essays in Richard Rorty, *Contingency, Irony, Solidarity* (Cambridge: Cambridge University Press, 1989) and *Objectivity, Relativism, and Truth*.

19. Alasdair MacIntyre, *After Virtue* (London: Duckworth, 1981).
20. See, for example, Brian Barry, 'How Not to Defend Liberal Institutions'.
21. For example, the freedom of speech which moved J. S. Mill to such eloquence was of no interest to Locke; the patterned distribution of income and wealth defended in the work of John Rawls has been rejected by Robert Nozick and other libertarians on the grounds that such patterns conflict with a commitment to equal individual liberty; the right to participate directly in general assemblies which Rousseau took to be so fundamental as a condition of political liberty is not found in so unmitigated a form in any other liberal writings.
22. The qualification that liberals are *normally* opposed to this ordering of values allows for a change of ordering in extreme and unusual conditions, for example, when national security is threatened, or in times of war. See, for example, John Rawls on the 'clear and present danger' rule, *Political Liberalism*, Lecture VII.
23. I would like to thank Hallvard Lillehammer for his help on this point: the resulting definitions are mine rather than his.
24. The terms of the debate about internalism were set by Bernard Williams, 'Internal and External Reasons', *Moral Luck* (Cambridge: Cambridge University Press, 1981). See also 'Internal Reasons and the Obscurity of Blame', *Making Sense of Humanity* (Cambridge: Cambridge University Press, 1995).
25. Derek Parfit defends a version of externalism in 'Reasons and Motivation', *Proceedings of the Aristotelian Society*, Supplementary Volume LXXI (1997), 99–130.
26. See, for example, Hallvard Lillehammer, 'The Doctrine of Internal Reasons', *The Journal of Value Inquiry*, **34**(4) (2000), 507–16, p. 507. See also T. M. Scanlon, *What We Owe to Each Other* (Cambridge, Mass.: Harvard University Press, 1998), 'Appendix'.
27. See, for example, Christine Korsgaard, 'Skepticism about Practical Reason', *Creating the Kingdom of Ends* (Cambridge: Cambridge University Press, 1996), pp. 311–34. See also Thomas Nagel, *The Possibility of Altruism* (Princeton, NJ.: Princeton University Press, 1978), Chapters 1 and 2.
28. See Joseph Raz, *The Morality of Freedom*.
29. The foundations of empiricist constructivism can be found in Harry Frankfurt, 'Freedom of the Will and the Concept of a Person', *The Importance of What We Care About* (Cambridge: Cambridge University Press, 1988).
30. Charles Taylor, 'What is Human Agency?' and 'The Concept of a Person', *Human Agency and Language: Philosophical Papers Vol. I* (Cambridge: Cambridge University Press, 1985).
31. Charles Taylor, 'Atomism', *Philosophy and the Human Sciences: Philosophical Papers Vol. II* (Cambridge: Cambridge University Press, 1985).
32. See Thomas E. Hill Jnr., *Dignity and Practical Reason in Kant's Moral Theory* (Ithaca: Cornell University Press, 1992), and 'Kantian Constructivism in Ethics', *Ethics*, **99**(1989), 752–70; Onora O'Neill, *Towards Justice and*

Virtue: A Constructive Account of Practical Reasoning (Cambridge: Cambridge University Press, 1996), and 'Constructivisms in Ethics', *Constructions of Reason: Explorations of Kant's Practical Philosophy* (Cambridge: Cambridge University Press, 1989).

33. Onora O'Neill, *Towards Justice and Virtue: A Constructive Account of Practical Reasoning*. See also *Constructions of Reason: Explorations of Kant's Practical Philosophy*.

2   Constructivism in Rawls

1. A maximin distribution of goods is one in which the worst outcome is superior to the worst outcome of all other distributions of that good. See John Rawls, *A Theory of Justice*, pp. 152 ff.
2. Ibid., p. 303.
3. In *Political Liberalism* this principle now distributes 'an equal claim to *a fully adequate scheme* of equal basic rights and liberties, which scheme is compatible with the same scheme for all; and in this scheme the equal political liberties, and only those liberties, are to be guaranteed their fair value' (p. 5). In *A Theory of Justice* the principle reads: 'Each person is to have an equal right to *the most extensive total system* of equal basic liberties compatible with a similar system of liberty for all' (p. 302), emphasis added.
4. In *A Theory of Justice* the emphasis is more on social primary goods as necessary means for the pursuit of diverse ends: instrumentally rational people would choose to have more rather than less of these goods. But in *Political Liberalism* the emphasis is more on social primary goods as providing the conditions in which persons can exercise their capacity for a conception of the good and their capacity for a sense of justice. For discussion see Onora O'Neill, 'Constructivisms in Ethics', *Constructions of Reason*.
5. See John Rawls, *A Theory of Justice*, p. 8, and *Political Liberalism*, pp. 284–5.
6. John Rawls, *Political Liberalism*, p. 90.
7. John Rawls, *A Theory of Justice*, pp. 136 ff.
8. John Rawls, *Political Liberalism*, p. 89.
9. Ibid., pp. 140–1.
10. Ibid., p. 64. See also pp. 140–2.
11. Thomas E. Hill, 'The Stability Problem in "Political Liberalism"', *Pacific Philosophical Quarterly*, **75** (1994), 333–52, p. 338.
12. Leif Wenar, '"Political Liberalism": An Internal Critique', *Ethics*, **106** (1995), 32–62, p. 33 and p. 61 respectively (emphases added). Wenar sometimes expresses the aim of justification in *Political Liberalism* in terms that retain an ambiguity between the 'likelihood' and the 'possibility' readings of stage 2, for example: 'The conception of justice that Rawls claims can be the focus of an overlapping consensus will not be acceptable to diverse comprehensive views as we know them and can expect them to become', p. 32 (emphasis added).
13. Leif Wenar, '"Political Liberalism": An Internal Critique', p. 45.

14. Ibid., p. 46.
15. Ibid., p. 41.
16. *Dogmatic Constitution on Divine Revelation*, article 6, cited in Leif Wenar, '*Political Liberalism*: An Internal Critique', p. 44, n. 20.
17. John Rawls, *Political Liberalism*, pp. 107–8.
18. Ibid., p. 108.
19. Ibid., p. 19.
20. Ibid., p. 19.
21. Ibid., pp. 19–20.
22. Ibid., p. 50.
23. Ibid., p. 79.
24. Ibid., p. 30.
25. Ibid., p. 32.
26. Ibid., p. 34.
27. Ibid., pp. 81–2.
28. Ibid., p. 86.
29. Ibid., p. 15.
30. Ibid., p. 16.
31. Ibid., p. 16.
32. Ibid., p. 16.
33. Ibid., p. 93. Rawls contrasts this complexity with the simplicity of the conception of the person as knower of moral truths involved in the acceptance of the Rational Intuitionism of, for example, G. E. Moore. See G. E. Moore, *Principia Ethica* (Cambridge: Cambridge University Press, 1986).
34. See John Rawls, *Political Liberalism*, p. 97.
35. All quoted material in a–f in Ibid., pp. 56–7.
36. (3) is Brian Barry's position. See *Justice As Impartiality* (Oxford: Clarendon Press, 1995), Chapter 7.
37. John Rawls, *Political Liberalism*, pp. 36–7, p. 144
38. David Estlund, 'Making Truth Safe for Democracy', *The Idea of Democracy* David Copp, Jean Hampton, and John E. Roemer (eds) (Cambridge: Cambridge University Press, 1993), p. 90.
39. John Rawls, *Political Liberalism*, p. 63.
40. Rawls claims that reasonable pluralism is 'in part the work of free practical reason within the framework of free institutions', and that, 'the fact of reasonable pluralism is not an unfortunate condition of human life'. Ibid., p. 37.
41 A modern democratic society is characterized not simply by a pluralism of comprehensive religious, philosophical, and moral doctrines but by a pluralism of incompatible yet reasonable comprehensive doctrines. No one of these doctrines is affirmed by citizens generally. Nor should one expect that in the foreseeable future one of them, or some other reasonable doctrine, will ever be affirmed by all, or nearly all, citizens. Political liberalism assumes that, for political purposes, a plurality of reasonable yet incompatible comprehensive doctrines is the normal result of the exercise of human reason within the framework of the free institutions of a constitutional democratic regime. John Rawls, *Political Liberalism*, p. xvi.

42. Ibid., p. 61.
43. Ibid., p. 61. For discussion of the way in which Rawls' and Barry's claims about the burdens of judgement figure in arguments for toleration see Susan Mendus and Matt Matravers, 'The Reasonableness of Pluralism', *Reasonable Tolerance: The Culture of Toleration in Diverse Societies* Catriona McKinnon and Dario Castiglione (eds).
44. John Rawls, *Political Liberalism*, p. 224.
45. Ibid., p. 226.
46. John Rawls, 'The Idea of Public Reason Revisited', *Collected Papers* (Cambridge, Mass.: Harvard University Press, 1999), p. 594, emphasis added.
47. Many theorists of deliberative democracy insist that political justification be limited to the specification of a procedural ideal for political institutions to mirror, and that any attempt to use this ideal as a position from which substantive principles can be justified is a mistake. See, for example, Joshua Cohen, 'Deliberation and Democratic Legitimacy', James Bohman and William Rehg (eds), *Deliberative Democracy: Essays on Reason and Politics* (Cambridge, Mass.: MIT Press, 1999). However, if the claim is not the utopian one that all persons must actually engage in deliberation structured by institutions mirroring the ideal for any principle to be justified, then it must be the case that some principles – if we are to have any at all – are arrived at by imaginatively reconstructing justifications in terms of the ideal procedure. In that case, why can't the ideal be used both as a model for institution building and as a touchstone for the justification of much-needed principles absent these institutions? Cf. Jürgen Habermas, 'Reconciliation Through the Use of Public Reason', *Journal of Philosophy*, **XCII**(3) (1995), 110–31.
48. See John Rawls, 'The Idea of Public Reason Revisited', p. 576.
49. Ibid., p. 577.
50. Ibid., p. 578.
51. John Rawls, *Political Liberalism*, p. 9.
52. The case is slightly complicated by Rawls' post-*Political Liberalism* paper, 'The Idea of Public Reason Revisited'. He claims here that public reason based guidelines of enquiry do not prevent us from 'introduc[ing] into political discussion at any time our comprehensive doctrine, religious or nonreligious, provided that, in due course, we give properly public reasons to support the principles and policies our comprehensive doctrine is said to support' (p. 584). Rawls refers to this aspect of public reason-based guideline as 'the proviso'. Because the proviso retains the demand that all reasons offered in political debate are *eventually* presented in public reason, it does not detract from the importance that *Political Liberalism* accords to public reason in political debate.
53. The term 'epistemic abstinence' is taken from Joseph Raz, 'Facing Diversity: The Case of Epistemic Abstinence', *Philosophy and Public Affairs*, **19**(1) (1990), 3–46.
54. John Rawls, *Political Liberalism*, p. 224.
55. John Rawls, *Justice as Fairness: A Restatement* (Cambridge, Mass.: Harvard University Press, 2001).

56. Thomas Hill thinks that acceptability to stage 2 persons is both necessary *and* sufficient for justificatory success. This means that he would reject the view that motivational adequacy must be tested not only in terms of the formal acceptability of stage 1 reasons, but also in terms of the demandingness of these reasons. This makes Hill's reading of Rawls more Kantian than mine. *Pace* Hill, making demandingness part of the test of motivational adequacy is not tantamount to treating stage 2 as a prediction, which can be seen from the fact that demandingness can be retained as part of this test while rejecting a reading of stage 2 like Wenar's. See Thomas E. Hill, 'The Stability Problem in "Political Liberalism"', especially p. 344.
57. John Rawls, 'Justice as Fairness: Political not Metaphysical', *Collected Papers*, p. 412. See also ibid., p. 390, 408, 411, 413.
58. For a classic account, see Isaiah Berlin, 'The Pursuit of the Ideal', *The Crooked Timber of Humanity*. For a better account see Joseph Raz, *The Morality of Freedom*, Chapter 13. For general discussion see Ruth Chang (ed.), *Incommensurability, Incomparability and Practical Reason* (Cambridge, Mass.: Harvard University Press, 1997).
59. See my 'Toleration and the Character of Pluralism', Catriona McKinnon and Dario Castiglione (eds), *Reasonable Tolerance: The Culture of Toleration in Diverse Societies*.
60. John Rawls, *Political Liberalism*, Lecture I. In this Lecture Rawls describes pluralism in terms of 'opposing and irreconcilable' (p. 3), and 'conflicting and irreconcilable' (p. 36) differences, rather than in terms of incommensurable differences.
61. John Rawls, *Political Liberalism*, p. 60. See also p. 54, 61, 81.
62. Ibid., p. 56.
63. Ibid., pp. 56–7.
64. See Brian Barry, *Justice as Impartiality*, Chapter 7.
65. The (probably apocryphal) story is this. In the questions session after having given a talk on cosmology in London, Bertrand Russell was asked – by a little old lady, so the story goes – how he knew that the Earth is not carried through the Universe on the back of a giant turtle. Russell replied, 'In that case, dear lady, what supports the turtle?' To which the little old lady replied, 'You may think you're very clever, young man, but it's turtles all the way down.'

3 Self-Respect

1. Robert Nozick, *Anarchy, State and Utopia* (Oxford: Blackwell, 1974), pp. 240–1.
2. These rewards often just take the form of social approval.
3. Robert Nozick, *Anarchy, State and Utopia*, p. 241.
4. The peculiarity of this idea is captured by Anthony Skillen in his claim that 'A boat builder is happy if his boat has what a boat needs; he

doesn't need a reserve army of incompetents to maintain his self-esteem.' Cited in Jonathan Wolff, *Robert Nozick: Property, Justice and the Minimal State* (Cambridge: Polity Press, 1991), p. 126.

5. Thomas E. Hill Jnr. acknowledges the importance of success according to individual criteria of excellence in his 'Self-Respect Reconsidered', *Autonomy and Self-Respect*. He claims that:

   a person can respect himself quite aside from acknowledging his merits and appreciating his rights. This form of self-respect would require that one develop and live by a set of personal standards by which one is prepared to judge oneself even if they are not extended to others … The sort of personal standards and ideals on which one's self-respect depends are typically seen as inescapably part of oneself. Whether one sees them as objective or not, one genuinely takes the attitude that one is, in one's own view, better or worse according to how one measures up to them. (pp. 22–3).

6. In making this point to me Matt Matravers compared individual standards of excellence with Philip Larkin's 'innate assumptions':

   … Where do these
   Innate assumptions come from? Not from what
   We think truest, or most want to do:
   Those warp-tight shut like doors. They're more a style
   Our lives bring with them: habit for a while,
   Suddenly they harden into all we've got.

7. See, for example, John Stuart Mill, *The Subjection of Women* (Indianapolis: Hackett Publishing Co., 1988). See also F. A. Hayek, *John Stuart Mill and Harriet Taylor: Their Correspondence and Subsequent Marriage* (Chicago: University of Chicago Press, 1951).

8. This example is taken from the made for TV film *The Stepford Wives*. Briefly, the story follows a young wife and mother who moves with her husband to the town of Stepford. There she finds that wives like herself entirely devote themselves to satisfying the needs of their husbands and children and attending the occasional perfectly organised barbecue in floral chiffon dresses. The young wife investigates and finds that the husbands of Stepford are co-conspirators in a plot which involves kidnapping their wives and replacing them with physically identical robots who do all the cooking, cleaning, flattering and entertaining that their recalcitrant human wives would not.

9. For a good discussion see Robin Dillon, 'How To Lose Your Self-Respect', *American Philosophical Quarterly*, **29**(2) (1992), 125–39.

10. This is the position Diana Meyers takes in *Self, Society and Personal Choice* (New York: Columbia University Press, 1988) when she states that:

    absorbing and following a socially enforced code manifests a natural capacity comparable to the ant's ability to carry heavy loads. When self-respect is based on this sort of adaptability rather than on a capacity for reflection and choice, self-respect is directed at a natural capability rather than at one's distinctive capacities as an agent. Thus this respect is unwarranted, and uncompromised self-respect requires the exercise of the complete range of one's moral faculties. (p. 226)

Another example of this approach can be found in Elizabeth Telfer's 'Self-Respect' (*Philosophical Quarterly*, Vol. 18 (1968), 115–21). She claims that:

When we say that someone has self-respect, we are attributing to him qualities of independence, tenacity and self-control. A man cannot have [conative] self-respect if he does not have these; whether he himself values them or not is immaterial. (p. 118)

11. See Jean Hampton's 'Selflessness and The Loss of Self' in *Altruism*, E. F. Paul, F. Miller and J. Paul (eds) (Cambridge: Cambridge University Press, 1993).
12. In *A Theory of Justice* Rawls continually and confusingly treats 'self-respect' and 'self-esteem' as synonyms. This supposed synonymy is absent in *Political Liberalism*.
13. Cited in Lawrence L. Thomas, 'Morality and Our Self-Concept', *Journal of Value Inquiry*, **12** (1978), 258–68, p. 258.
14. For an excellent discussion of the distinction between self-respect and self-esteem see David Sachs, 'How to Distinguish Self-Respect from Self-Esteem', *Philosophy and Public Affairs*, **10**(4) (1981), 346–60. Also helpful is Stephen J. Massey, 'Is Self-Respect a Moral or a Psychological Concept?', *Ethics*, **93** (1983), 246–61, and Michael Walzer, *Spheres of Justice* (Oxford: Martin Robertson, 1983), pp. 272–80.
15. For a similar account of this relationship see Chapter 1 of Thomas E. Hill's *Autonomy and Self-Respect*. Hill's account differs from mine in that he defines servility in terms of a person's failure to appreciate the importance of, or perhaps even to acknowledge the existence of, her rights.
16. Bobby Sands was the first of ten IRA hunger-strikers to die in the H-Blocks on 5 May 1981.
17. I am grateful to Tim Oakley and Robert Young at LaTrobe University, Melbourne for helpful discussion of this point.
18. One objection to a counterfactual account of subservience is that the counterfactuals are hard to run, which makes it difficult to judge whether a person is or is not subservient. In response, (a) this is a problem with respect to counterfactual accounts of anything, and (b) it could be seen as a virtue of the account: judgements about whether persons are subservient *are* hard to make. But this does not mean that we cannot use the counterfactual account when we are thinking about how social structures promote or impede the development of self-respect. We assess these structures according to whether they would inhibit or thwart a person's expectations that others give her reasons for their demands regardless of whether we can tell whether any particular person would have such expectations, and this is all we need.

19. John Rawls, *A Theory of Justice*, p. 440. Rawls repeatedly stresses the significance of self-respect throughout his work. See also *A Theory of Justice* pp. 92, 107, 443, 543–45, and *Political Liberalism* pp. 106, 203, 318, 319.
20. John Rawls, *A Theory of Justice*, p. 440.
21. Ibid., p. 440.
22. Ibid., p. 408.
23. Ibid., p. 417.
24. Ibid., p. 426. The Aristotelian principle also has a 'companion effect' which is that:

As we witness the exercise of well-trained abilities of others, these displays are enjoyed by us and arouse a desire that we should be able to do the same things ourselves. We want to be like those persons who can exercise the abilities we find latent in our nature. (p. 428)

The companion effect will become important in the arguments of the next chapter.
25. The extent of Rawls' reliance on community as a provider of self-respect supporting benefits is especially well brought out by Daniel Brudney in 'Community and Completion', Andrews Reath, Barbara Herman and Christine M. Korsgaard (eds) *Reclaiming the History of Ethics: Essays for John Rawls* (Cambridge: Cambridge University Press, 1997).
26. John Rawls, *A Theory of Justice*, p. 441.
27. Ibid., p. 441.
28. Ibid., p. 441.
29. In *A Theory of Justice* Rawls defines the excellences as non-exclusive goods in the sense that 'the excellences are a condition of human flourishing; they are goods from everyone's point of view' (p. 443). If a person has excellences pertinent to her plans and projects, whether they be natural or cultivated talents or virtues, then she will have the confidence to pursue those projects and find that, in virtue of how she satisfies the Aristotelian principle in this pursuit, she receives the self-respect supporting esteem of others. As Rawls says, the excellences:

enable us to carry out a more satisfying plan of life enhancing our sense of mastery. At the same time, these attributes are appreciated by those with whom we associate, and the pleasure they take in our person and in what we do supports our self-esteem (p. 444)

30. John Rawls, *A Theory of Justice*, p. 440.
31. The claim that Rawls' commitment to participation in communities of shared interests as a social condition of self-respect implies commitment to social criteria of excellence as contributing to self-respect has generated misplaced criticisms of Rawls' conception of self-respect. For example, see Robert Yanal, 'Self-Esteem', *Noûs*, **21** (1987), 363–79, who attacks the idea that success according to social criteria is necessary for self-respect,

and Lawrence L. Thomas, 'Morality and Our Self-Concept', who attacks the idea that such success is sufficient for self-respect.
32. 'All social primary goods – liberty and opportunity, income and wealth, and the bases of self-respect – are to be distributed equally unless an unequal distribution of any or all of these goods is to the advantage of the least favoured', John Rawls, *A Theory of Justice*, p. 303.
33. John Rawls, *A Theory of Justice*, p. 62.
34. John Rawls, *Political Liberalism*, p. 76.
35. John Rawls, *A Theory of Justice*, p. 319. This description of the social bases of self-respect is also affirmed in *Political Liberalism* where Rawls claims that:

> The social bases of self-respect are explained by the structure and content of just institutions together with features of the public political culture, such as the recognition and acceptance of principles of justice. (p. 181)

36. John Rawls, *A Theory of Justice*, p. 440. See also ibid., p. 92, p. 107, p. 443 and pp. 543–5.
37. John Rawls, *Political Liberalism*, p. 318.
38. Ibid., p. 319. See also ibid., p. 106 and p. 203.
39. The reason why self-respect appears in justice-justification *via* the *social bases* of self-respect is that self-respect *per se* is, like good health, a natural primary good, and so not amenable to social distribution. See *A Theory of Justice*, p. 62.
40. John Rawls, *Political Liberalism*, p. 291.
41. John Rawls, *A Theory of Justice*, p. 544.
42. Joshua Cohen, 'Democratic Equality', *Ethics*, **99** (1989), 727–51.
43. Joshua Cohen, 'Democratic Equality', p. 737.

4 Reasoning about Justice

1. The sense in which subservience damages a person's ability to give and receive political justifications is captured in Thomas E. Hill's figure of 'Uncle Tom', whose servility is a defect from this point of view because it prevents him from asserting his rights in justificatory debate with those to whom he defers. See Thomas E. Hill Jnr, 'Servility and Self-Respect' in his *Autonomy and Self-Respect*. The damage to justificatory status incurred by subservience is also captured by Kant when he remarks that, '[O]ne who makes himself a worm cannot complain afterwards if people step on him'. 'Metaphysical First Principles of the Doctrine of Virtue', Part I, §V, *The Metaphysics of Morals*, ed. Mary Gregor (Cambridge: Cambridge University Press, 1996), p. 188.
2. Charles Taylor, 'What is Human Agency?', *Human Agency and Language: Philosophical Papers I*. What follows is an adaptation of Taylor, not a reproduction, primarily because I do not endorse Taylor's conception of reasons as given just by desires. A desire may give a person a reason to act,

but it is not part of my account – as it is of Taylor's – that a desire becomes such a reason only when it is evaluated in terms of some other, second-order, desire.

3. See Charles Taylor, 'What is Human Agency?', pp. 23–4.
4. Ibid., pp. 16–17.
5. Ibid., p. 19. Taylor argues that the capacity for strong evaluation characterises human agency *per se*. I shall only be concerned to defend the much weaker claim that strong evaluation characterises practical reasoning about questions of justice.
6. Ibid., p. 21.
7. Kant, 'Metaphysical First Principles of the Doctrine of Virtue', Part I, SXVII, *The Metaphysics of Morals*, p. 167.
8. See Ronald Dworkin, 'Equality and Capability', in *Sovereign Virtue* (Cambridge, Mass.: Harvard University Press, 2000); see also the next section.
9. The pastry example comes from Charles Taylor, 'What is Human Agency?', p. 17.
10. Ibid., p. 24.
11. Cf. John Rawls, *Political Liberalism*, p. 31.
12. Note the qualification 'might' in this sentence. I am not proposing that it is always appropriate for people to lower their standards in the face of their failure to meet them: this would make the achievement of self-respect far too easy, and meaningless. Rather, all I want to allow for is the possibility of such cases.
13. In 'What is Human Agency?', Taylor claims that,

The notion of identity refers us to certain evaluations which are essential because they are the indispensable horizon or foundation out of which we reflect and evaluate as persons. To lose this horizon, or not to have found it, is indeed a terrifying experience of disaggregation and loss. This is why we can speak of an 'identity-crisis' when we have lost our grip on who we are. (p. 35).

Taylor claims that a person without such horizons, 'would be utterly without identity...a kind of extensionless point, a pure leap into the void' (p. 35), and that the Existentialist doctrine of radical choice relies on such a conception of the person, and is thus to be rejected.
14. Ronald Dworkin, 'Equality and Capability', in *Sovereign Virtue*, p. 291.
15. Ibid., p. 292.
16. Ibid., p. 293. It is not clear whether Dworkin thinks that none of our preferences and desires are tools for achieving buzzes and ticks. Whether or not this is his view, it seems implausibly strong. What is wrong with the claim that *some* preferences and desires are buzz and tick generating instruments?
17. Of course, the question of what counts as a basic question of justice will be disputed. But that is not to the point here. If the distinction can be

made, then it is possible to see questions like these as falling on either side of the divide, and then to think that different sorts of practical reasoning are appropriate for each side. Cf. Matt Matravers, *Justice and Punishment: The Rationale of Coercion* (Oxford: Oxford University Press, 2000), pp. 114–18.

18. For discussion see Bernard Williams, *Morality: An Introduction to Ethics* (Cambridge: Cambridge University Press, 1972), Chapter 1; Joseph Raz, 'The Amoralist', *Ethics and Practical Reason*, Garrett Cullity and Berys Gaut (eds) (Oxford: Clarendon Press, 1997).

19. For explorations of the relationship between toleration and reasonableness see Catriona McKinnon and Dario Castiglione (eds), *Reasonable Tolerance: The Culture of Toleration in Diverse Societies.*

20. John Rawls, 'The Idea of Public Reason Revisited', p. 594, emphasis added.

21. Ibid., *passim.*

22. Ibid., p. 576.

23. Ibid., p. 577.

24. Ibid., p. 578.

25. 'The ideal of democratic citizens trying to conduct their political affairs on terms supported by public values that we might reasonably expect others to endorse ... expresses a willingness to listen to what others have to say and being ready to accept reasonable accommodations or alterations in one's view.' John Rawls, *Political Liberalism*, p. 253.

26. For a defence of this Millean conception of civility see Richard C. Sinopoli, 'Thick-Skinned Liberalism: Redefining Civility', *American Political Science Review*, **89**(3) (1995), 612–20.

27. John Rawls, *A Theory of Justice*, p. 428. For a critique of Rawls' account of how self-respect depends on achieving ends in accord with the Aristotelian principle see Robert Yanal, 'Self-Esteem', and Larry L. Thomas, 'Morality and Our Self-Concept'.

28. Cf. Rawls on 'the morality of association', *A Theory of Justice*, pp. 468–9. Cf. also Barry Barnes, 'Tolerance as a Primary Virtue', *Res Publica*, **7**(3) (2001), 231–45.

29. See Sarah Buss, 'Appearing Respectful: The Moral Significance of Manners', *Ethics*, **109** (1999), 795–826. See also Nancy Rosenblum, *Membership and Morals: The Personal Uses of Pluralism in America* (Princeton, NJ.: Princeton University Press, 1998). Judith Shklar's discussion of the social value of hypocrisy also invokes skills similar to the skills of civility, 'Let Us Not Be Hypocritical', *Ordinary Vices* (Cambridge, Mass.: Belknap Press, 1984). For a related discussion of the importance of protecting conventions of politeness see Thomas Nagel, 'Concealment and Exposure', *Philosophy and Public Affairs*, **27**(1) (1998), 3–30.

30. For a version of this argument see David Miller, 'Citizenship and Pluralism', *Political Studies*, **43**(3) (1995), 432–50.

31. John Rawls, *A Theory of Justice*, p. 338. See also ibid., p. 319; *Political Liberalism*, p. 181.

5   The Social Bases of Self-Respect

1. John Rawls, *A Theory of Justice*, p. 319.
2. Ibid., p. 303.
3. Rawls' two principles of justice as they appear in *A Theory of Justice*, with associated priority rules, are as follows:

First Principle
Each person is to have an equal right to the most extensive total system of equal basic liberties compatible with a similar system of liberty for all.

Second Principle
Social and economic inequalities are to be arranged so that they are both:
(a) to the greatest benefit of the least advantaged, consistent with the just savings principle, and
(b) attached to offices and positions open to all under conditions of fair equality of opportunity.

First Priority Rule (The Priority of Liberty)
The principles of justice are to be ranked in lexical order and therefore liberty can be restricted only for the sake of liberty. There are two cases:
(a) a less extensive liberty must strengthen the total system of liberty shared by all;
(b) a less than equal liberty must be acceptable to those with the lesser liberty.

Second Priority Rule (The Priority of Justice over Efficiency and Welfare)
The second principle of justice is lexically prior to the principle of efficiency and to that of maximising the sum of advantages; and fair opportunity is prior to the difference principle. There are two cases:
(a) an inequality of opportunity must enhance the opportunities of those with the lesser opportunity;
(b) an excessive rate of saving must on balance mitigate the burden of those bearing this hardship.
(John Rawls, *A Theory of Justice*, pp. 302–3)

The main difference between the special conception of justice as presented in *A Theory of Justice* and as presented in *Political Liberalism* relates to the first principle. In the later work, Rawls refers not to the 'the most extensive total system of equal basic liberties', but rather to 'the most fully adequate scheme of equal basic liberties'. See *Political Liberalism*, p. 291.
4. As noted in Chapter 3, this account is inspired by Joshua Cohen's taxonomy in 'Democratic Equality'.
5. John Rawls, *A Theory of Justice*, p. 442, emphasis added.
6. As I allowed in the last chapter, this is not always the case: some people can find support for their self-respect in associational life without active engagement in public reason. However, I think such cases are not the norm, and even in such cases, a self-respecting person is still committed

to endorsing public reason, in the sense of not attempting to dismantle or disrupt procedures governed by the ideal of public reason, because such procedures make possible her future movement to a different group providing the associational bases of self-respect.

7. See Henry Shue, 'Liberty and Self-Respect', *Ethics*, **85** (1975), 195–203.
8. John Rawls, *A Theory of Justice*, pp. 544–5. For similar arguments see Thomas E. Hill Jnr, 'Servility and Self-Respect'; Lawrence L. Thomas, 'Self-Respect: Theory and Practice', Robin Dillon (ed.), *Dignity, Character, and Self-Respect* (New York: Routledge, 1995); Joel Feinberg, 'The Nature and Value of Rights', *Journal of Value Inquiry*, **4** (1970), 243–60; Ronald Dworkin, 'Justice and Rights', *Taking Rights Seriously* (London: Duckworth, 1977); Avishai Margalit, *The Decent Society* (Cambridge, Mass.: Harvard University Press, 1996), Chapter 2.
9. On pornography and censorship see the debate between Ronald Dworkin and Catherine MacKinnon. Ronald Dworkin, 'Women and Pornography', *New York Review of Books*, 21 October 1993, 36–42; Catherine MacKinnon, *Only Words* (Cambridge, Mass.: Harvard University Press, 1993) and 'Pornography: An Exchange', *New York Review of Books*, 3 March 1994, 47–9. On questions about the censorship of literature and art raised by the Rushdie affair see Jeremy Waldron, 'Rushdie and Religion', *Liberal Rights* (Cambridge: Cambridge University Press, 1993); Tariq Modood, 'Muslims, Incitement to Hatred, and the Law', John Horton (ed.), *Liberalism, Multiculturalism, and Toleration* (Basingstoke: Macmillan – now Palgrave Macmillan, 1993); and Peter Jones, 'Respecting Beliefs and Rebuking Rushdie', ibid.
10. Although see Stuart White, 'Freedom of Association and the Right to Exclude', *Journal of Political Philosophy*, 5(4) (1997), 373–91.
11. Cf. John Rawls, *Political Liberalism*, p. 199.
12. See, for example, Will Kymlicka, *Liberalism, Community and Culture* (Oxford: Clarendon Press, 1995) and Joseph Raz, 'Multiculturalism', *Ethics in the Public Domain* (Oxford: Clarendon Press, 1994).
13. However, it is worth remarking that it is not clear that a concern to maximin the social bases of self-respect can lend support to special measures to protect *cultural* groups, over and above any group providing the associational bases of self-respect. A clear version of this criticism can be found in John Tomasi, 'Kymlicka, Liberalism and Respect for Cultural Minorities', *Ethics*, **105** (1995), 580–603.
14. The material in the remainder of this section is adapted from my 'Exclusion Rules and Self-Respect', *The Journal of Value Inquiry*, **34** (2000) 491–505. In this paper I propose a solution to the problem I outline here.
15. *Roberts* v. *United States Jaycees*, 468 US 609 (1984). The Jaycees are a national organisation in the US with local associations devoted to fund raising and performing activities of benefit to the local community, much like the Rotary Club. Until the Supreme Court decision in 1984 the Jaycees were a fraternal society, and admitted only men between the ages of eighteen and thirty-five to full membership (although women were admitted as 'associates'). The Jaycees defended their exclusion rule on the

grounds that they were an association devoted to promoting the interests of young men.

16. The Basic Income European Network, founded in 1986 to promote Europe-wide discussion of UBI, defines it as: an income unconditionally paid to all on an individual basis, without means test or work requirement. The Citizen's Income Trust (http://www.citizens-income.org.uk), which evolved out of the Basic Income Research Group (founded 1984) and is devoted to the promotion of UBI as a social security reform, defines UBI as an income paid by the state to every man, woman and child as a right of citizenship.

17. For detailed versions of these arguments see my, 'Unconditional Basic Income and the Reciprocity Objection: or, Should Scroungers be Fed?', work in progress. For a good general review of various arguments for UBI see Philippe Van Parijs (ed.), *Arguing for Basic Income* (London: Verso, 1992).

18. See Hermione Parker, *Instead of the Dole* (London: Routledge, 1989).

19. Stuart White, 'Liberal Equality, Exploitation, and the Case for an Unconditional Basic Income', *Political Studies*, **45**(2) (1997), 312–26, p. 318.

20. Stuart White, 'Liberal Equality, Exploitation, and the case for an Unconditional Basic Income', p. 320. Van Parijs' responds to White in 'Reciprocity and the Justification of an Unconditional Basic Income. Reply to Stuart White', *Political Studies*, **45**(2) (1997), 327–30.

21. For analysis of the mess that the literature is in see Matt Matravers, 'Responsibility, Luck, and the "Equality of What?" Debate', *Political Studies* (2002), forthcoming.

22. In particular, see Elizabeth Anderson, 'What is the Point of Equality?', *Ethics*, **109** (1999), 287–337.

23. A prime example of this clash is found in Rawls. Rawls repeatedly and everywhere says that self-respect is the most important of the primary goods, and yet he explicitly rejects UBI using a reciprocity objection to it. See *Political Liberalism*, pp. 181–2, n. 9.

24. Richard Norman, 'The Social Basis of Equality', Andrew Mason (ed.), *Ideals of Equality* (Oxford: Blackwell, 1998).

25. Richard Norman, 'The Social Basis of Equality', p. 40. See also David Miller on 'social equality', 'Equality and Justice', Andrew Mason (ed.), *Ideals of Equality*, pp. 21–36.

26. A Pareto-optimal distribution of x is a distribution in which no person could be made better off in terms of x without someone else being made worse off in terms of x; Pareto-optimality in the distribution of x is consistent with large x-inequalities.

27. As I stressed in note 6, this is not inconsistent with the claim made in the last chapter that some people do not find opportunity for self-respect through such active participation.

28. David Miller, 'Equality and Justice', p. 24. Miller claims that although social equality his distributive implications, it is not itself a matter of

distributive justice: the demands of distributive justice understood, for example, in terms of desert might come apart from the demands of social equality, which might not permit the inequalities demanded by a desert-based conception of distributive justice. Here I disagree with Miller. If self-respect provides the context for justice-oriented practical reasoning, and if social inequality can destroy opportunity for self-respect by destroying the framework/recognitional bases of self-respect, then social inequality is a matter of justice because it can shrink membership of the constituency of justification, and on a liberal view, unless membership is inclusive, the outcome of justificatory debate cannot be just.

Bibliography

Anderson, E., 'What is the Point of Equality?', *Ethics*, **109** (1999), 287–337.

Antony, L. M., and Witt, C. (eds), *A Mind of One's Own: Feminist Essays on Reason and Objectivity* (Boulder: Westview Press, 1993).

Arneson, R. J., 'Meaningful Work and Market Socialism', *Ethics*, **97** (1987), 517–45.

Arneson, R. J., 'Introduction' to 'Symposium on Rawlsian Theory of Justice: Some Recent Developments', *Ethics*, **99** (1989), 695–710.

Arneson, R. J., 'A Defence of Equal Opportunity for Welfare', *Philosophical Studies*, **62** (1991), 187–95.

Arneson, R. J., 'Is Socialism Dead? A Comment on Market Socialism and Basic Income Capitalism', *Ethics*, **102** (1992), 485–511.

Arneson, R. J., 'Egalitarianism and the Undeserving Poor', *Journal of Political Philosophy*, **5**(4) (1997), 327–50.

Avens, O., 'Rethinking Rights at Work', unpublished MS presented at Meeting of American Political Science Association, Washington DC, August 1997.

Baier, K., 'Justification in Ethics', see in *Justification: Nomos XXVIII* J. R. Pennock and J. W. Chapman (eds).

Baier, K., 'Justice and the Aims of Political Philosophy', *Ethics*, **99** (1989), 771–90.

Barber, B., 'Justifying Justice: Problems of Psychology, Politics and Measurement in Rawls', see in *Reading Rawls*, N. Daniels (ed).

Baron, M., 'Servility, Critical Deference and The Deferential Wife', *Philosophical Studies*, **48** (1985).

Baron, M., *Kantian Ethics Almost Without Apology* (Ithaca: Cornell University Press, 1995).

Barry, B., *Theories of Justice* (London: Harvester-Wheatsheaf, 1989).

Barry, B., *Liberty and Justice: Essays in Political Theory II* (Oxford: Clarendon Press, 1991).

Barry, B., *Justice As Impartiality* (Oxford: Clarendon Press, 1995).

Barry, B., 'The Attractions of Basic Income', see in J. Franklin (ed.), *Equality*.

Beiner, R., and Booth, W. J. (eds), *Kant and Political Philosophy* (New Haven: Yale University Press, 1993).

Beitz, C. R., 'Social and Cosmopolitan Liberalism', *International Affairs*, **75**(3) (1999), 515–29.

Bellamy, R., and Mason, A., (eds), *Political Concepts* (Manchester: Manchester University Press, 2002).

Berlin, I., *Four Essays On Liberty* (Oxford: Oxford University Press, 1969).

Berlin, I., *The Crooked Timber of Humanity* (London: Fontana Press, 1990).

Bertram, C., 'Political Justification, Theoretical Complexity, and Democratic Community', *Ethics*, **107**(4) (1997), 563–83.

Bertram, C., 'Theories of Public Reason', *Imprints*, **2**(1) (1997), 72–85.

Bird, C. C., 'Mutual Respect and Neutral Justification', *Ethics*, **107** (1996), 62–96.

Bohman, J., and Rehg, W. (eds), *Deliberative Democracy: Essays on Reason and Politics* (Cambridge, Mass.: MIT Press, 1999).

Boxill, B. R., 'Self-Respect and Protest', *Philosophy and Public Affairs*, **6** (1976), 58–69.

Brecher, B., *Getting What You Want? A Critique of Liberal Morality* (London: Routledge, 1998).

Brink, D. O., 'Rawlsian Constructivism in Moral Theory', *Canadian Journal of Philosophy*, **17**(1) (1987), 71–90.

Brink, D. O., *Moral Realism and the Foundations of Ethics* (Cambridge: Cambridge University Press, 1989).

Browning-Cole, E., and Coultrap-McQuinn, S. (eds), *Explorations in Feminist Ethics: Theory and Practice* (Bloomington: Indiana University Press, 1992).

Brudney, D., 'Community and Completion', see in A. Reath, B. Herman and C. M. Korsgaard (eds), *Reclaiming the History of Ethics: Essays for John Rawls*.

Buchanan, A. E., 'Assessing the Communitarian Critique of Liberalism', *Ethics*, **99** (1989), 852–82.

Buss, S., 'Appearing Respectful: The Moral Significance of Manners', *Ethics*, **109** (1999), 795–826.

Byrne, S. E., *A Rawlsian Argument for Basic Income* (MA Thesis, Dept. of Politics, University College Dublin, 1993).

Chang, R. (ed.), *Incommensurability, Incomparability and Practical Reason* (Cambridge, Mass.: Harvard University Press, 1997).

Cohen, J., 'Democratic Equality', *Ethics*, **99** (1989), 727–51.

Cohen, J., 'Moral Pluralism and Political Consensus', see in D. Copp, J. Hampton and J. E. Roemer (eds), *The Idea of Democracy*.

Cohen, J., 'A More Democratic Liberalism', *Michigan Law Review*, **92** (1994), 1503–46.

Cohen, J., 'The Arc of the Moral Universe', *Philosophy and Public Affairs*, **26**(2) (1996), 91–134.

Cohen, G. A., 'On the Currency of Egalitarian Justice', *Ethics*, **99** (1989), 906–44.

Cohen, G. A., 'Back to Socialist Basics', see in J. Franklin (ed.), *Equality*.

Cohen, G. A., 'Where the Action is: On the Site of Distributive Justice', *Philosophy and Public Affairs*, **26**(1) (1997), 3–30.

Cohen, G. A., *If You're an Egalitarian, How Come You're So Rich?* (Cambridge, Mass.: Harvard University Press, 2000).

Copp, D., 'Could Political Truth be a Hazard for Democracy?', see in D. Copp, J. Hampton and J. E. Roemer (eds), *The Idea of Democracy*.

Copp, D., Hampton, J., and Roemer, J. E. (eds), *The Idea of Democracy* (Cambridge: Cambridge University Press, 1993).

Cullity, G., and Gaut, B. (eds), *Ethics and Practical Reason* (Oxford: Clarendon Press, 1997).

D'Agostino, F., *Free Public Reason: Making It Up As We Go* (Oxford: Oxford University Press, 1996).

Dancy, J., *Moral Reasons* (Oxford: Blackwell, 1993).

Dancy, J., 'Why There is Really No Such Thing as the Theory of Motivation', *Proceedings of the Aristotelian Society*, **XCV** (1995), 1–19.

Daniels, N. (ed.), *Reading Rawls* (Stanford: Stanford University Press, 1989).

Daniels, N., *Justice and Justification: Reflective Equilibrium in Theory and Practice* (Cambridge: Cambridge University Press, 1996).

Darwall, S. L., 'Two Kinds of Respect', *Ethics*, **88** (1977), 36–49.

Deigh, J., 'Shame and Self-Esteem: A Critique', *Ethics*, **93** (1983), 225–45.

DePaul, M. R., 'Reflective Equilibrium and Foundationalism', *American Philosophical Quarterly*, **23**(1) (1986), 59–67.

Dillon, R. S., 'How To Lose Your Self-Respect', *American Philosophical Quarterly*, **29**(2) (1992), 125–39.

Dillon, R. S., 'Care and Respect', see in E. Browning-Cole and S. Coultrap-McQuinn (eds), *Explorations in Feminist Ethics: Theory and Practice*.

Dillon, R. S., 'Respect and Care: Toward Moral Integration', *Canadian Journal of Philosophy*, **22**(1) (1992), 105–32.

Dillon, R. S. (ed.), *Dignity, Character and Self-Respect* (New York: Routledge, 1995).

Dillon, R. S., 'Towards a Feminist Conception of Self-Respect', see in R. S. Dillon (ed.), *Dignity, Character and Self-Respect*.

Dillon, R. S., 'Self-Respect: Moral, Emotional, Political', *Ethics*, **107** (2) (1997), 226–49.

Dobson, A., and Stanyer, J. (eds), *Contemporary Political Studies*, 1998, Vol. 2 (Proceedings of the Political Studies Association Annual Conference, 1998).

Doppelt, G., 'Rawls' System of Justice: A Critique from the Left', *Noûs*, **15** (1981), 259–307.

Doppelt, G., 'Is Rawls's Kantian Liberalism Coherent and Defensible?', *Ethics*, **99** (1989), 815–51.

Dworkin, G., *The Theory and Practice of Autonomy* (Cambridge: Cambridge University Press, 1988).

Dworkin, G., 'Non-Neutral Principles', see in N. Daniels (ed.), *Reading Rawls*.

Dworkin, R., *Taking Rights Seriously* (London: Duckworth, 1977).

Dworkin, R., 'Women and Pornography', *New York Review of Books*, 21 October (1993), 36–42.

Dworkin, R., and MacKinnon, C., 'Pornography: An Exchange', *New York Review of Books*, 3 March (1994), 47–9.

Dworkin, R., 'Objectivity and Truth: You'd Better Believe It', *Philosophy and Public Affairs*, **25**(2) (1996), 87–139.

Dworkin, R., *Sovereign Virtue: The Theory and Practice of Equality* (Cambridge, Mass.: Harvard University Press, 2000).

Estlund, D., 'Making Truth Safe for Democracy', see in D. Copp, J. Hampton and J. E. Roemer (eds), *The Idea of Democracy*.

Estlund, D., 'The Insularity of the Reasonable: Why Political Liberalism Must Admit the Truth', *Ethics*, **108** (1998), 252–75.

Feinberg, J., 'The Nature and Value of Rights', *Journal of Value Inquiry*, **4** (1970), 243–60.

Fishkin, J., 'Liberal Theory and the Problem of Justification', see in J. R. Pennock and J. W. Chapman (eds), *Justification: Nomos XXVII*.

Frankfurt, H. G., *The Importance of What We Care About* (Cambridge: Cambridge University Press, 1988).

Franklin, J. (ed.), *Equality* (London: IPPR, 1997).

Freeman, S., 'Reason and Agreement in Social Contract Views', *Philosophy and Public Affairs*, **29**(2) (1990), 122–57.

Freeman, S., 'Contractualism, Moral Motivation, and Practical Reason', *Journal of Philosophy*, **LXXXVIII**(6) (1991), 281–303.

Friedman, M., 'Moral Integrity and the Deferential Wife', *Philosophical Studies*, **47** (1985), 141–50.

Gaus, G. F., *Value and Justification* (Cambridge: Cambridge University Press, 1990).

Gaus, G. F., *Justificatory Liberalism* (New York: Oxford University Press, 1996).

Galston, W. A., 'Defending Liberalism', *American Political Science Review*, **76** (1982), 621–9.

Galston, W. A., 'Pluralism and Social Unity', *Ethics*, **99** (1989), 711–26.

Galston, W. A., 'Two Concepts of Liberalism', *Ethics*, **105** (1995), 516–34.

Geras, N., *Solidarity in the Conversation of Humankind: The Ungroundable Liberalism of Richard Rorty* (London: Verso, 1995).

Gewirth, A., 'The Rationality of Reasonableness', *Synthese*, **57** (1983), 225–47.

Gibbard, A., 'Constructing Justice', *Philosophy and Public Affairs*, **20**(3) (1991).

Gilligan, C., *In a Different Voice: Psychological Theory and Women's Development* (Cambridge, Mass.: Harvard University Press, 1982).

Golding, M. P., 'The Nature of Compromise', see in J. R. Pennock and J. W. Chapman (eds), *Nomos XXI: Compromise in Ethics, Law and Politics*.

Goodin, R. E., and Reeve, A. (eds), *Liberal Neutrality* (London: Routledge, 1989).

Goodin, R. E., and Pettit, P., *A Companion to Contemporary Political Philosophy* (Oxford: Blackwell, 1993).

Gorz, A., 'On the Difference Between Society and Community, and Why Basic Income by Itself Cannot Confer Full Membership of Either', see in P. Van Parijs (ed.), *Arguing for Basic Income*.

Govier, T., 'Self-Trust, Autonomy and Self-Esteem', *Hypatia*, **8**(1) (1993), 99–120.

Gutmann, A., 'Communitarian Critics of Liberalism', *Philosophy and Public Affairs*, **14** (1985), 308–22.

Gutmann, A., and Thompson, D., *Democracy and Disagreement* (Cambridge, Mass.: Harvard University Press, 1996).

Habermas, J., 'Reconciliation Through the Use of Public Reason: Remarks on John Rawls's *Political Liberalism*', *The Journal of Philosophy*, **XCII**(3) (1995), 109–32.

Hampton, J., 'Should Political Philosophy be Done without Metaphysics?', *Ethics*, **99** (1989), 791–814.

Hampton, J., 'Feminist Contractarianism', see in L. M. Antony and C. Witt (eds), *A Mind of One's Own: Feminist Essays on Reason and Objectivity*.

Hampton, J., 'Selflessness and Loss of the Self', see in E. F. Paul, F. Miller and J. Paul (eds) *Altruism*.

Hampton, J., 'The Common Faith of Liberalism', *Pacific Philosophical Quarterly*, **75** (1994), 187–216.

Hampton, J., 'The Wisdom of the Egoist: The Moral and Political Implications of Valuing the Self', *Social Philosophy and Policy*, **14**(1) (1997), 21–51.

Hart, H. L. A., 'Rawls on Liberty and its Priority', see in N. Daniels (ed.), *Reading Rawls*.

Hayek, F. A., *John Stuart Mill and Harriet Taylor: Their Correspondence and Subsequent Marriage* (Chicago: University of Chicago Press, 1951).

Held, V., 'Reasonable Progress and Self-Respect', *Monist*, **57** (1973), 12–27.

Herzog, D., *Happy Slaves* (Chicago: University of Chicago Press, 1989).

Hill Jnr., T. E., 'Kantian Constructivism in Ethics', *Ethics*, **99** (1989), 752–70.

Hill Jnr., T. E., *Autonomy and Self-Respect* (Cambridge: Cambridge University Press, 1991).

Hill Jnr., T. E., *Dignity and Practical Reason in Kant's Moral Theory* (Ithaca: Cornell University Press, 1992).

Hill Jnr., T. E., 'Beneficence and Self-Love: A Kantian Perspective', see in E. F. Paul, F. Miller and J. Paul (eds), *Altruism*.

Hill Jnr., T. E., 'The Stability Problem in "Political Liberalism"', *Pacific Philosophical Quarterly*, **75** (1994), 333–52.

Hill Jnr, T. E., 'Reasonable Self-Interest', *Social Philosophy and Policy*, **14**(1) (1997), 52–85.

Horton, J. (ed.), *Liberalism, Multiculturalism and Toleration* (Basingstoke: Macmillan – now Palgrave Macmillan, 1993).

Hurka, T., 'Review of Sher, George. *Beyond Neutrality: Perfectionism and Politics*', *Ethics*, **109**(1) (1998), 187–90.

Jones, C., *Global Justice: Defending Cosmopolitanism* (Oxford: Oxford University Press, 1999).

Jones, P., 'The Idea of the Neutral State', see in R. E. Goodin and A. Reeve (eds), *Liberal Neutrality*.

Jones, P., 'Respecting Beliefs and Rebuking Rushdie', see in J. Horton (ed.), *Liberalism, Multiculturalism and Toleration*.

Kant, I., *Lectures on Ethics* (New York: Harper & Row Publishers, 1963).

Kant, I., *The Metaphysics of Morals*, Mary Gregor (ed.) (Cambridge: Cambridge University Press, 1996).

Kekes, J., 'Shame and Moral Progress', *Midwest Studies in Philosophy*, **XIII** (1988), 282–96.

Keshen, R., *Reasonable Self-Esteem* (Montreal: McGill-Queen's University Press, 1996).

Kolnai, A., 'Dignity', see in R. S. Dillon (ed.), *Dignity, Character and Self-Respect*.

Kneller, J., and Axinn, S. (eds), *Autonomy and Community: Readings in Contemporary Kantian Social Philosophy* (New York: State University of New York Press, 1998).

Korsgaard, C. M., *The Sources of Normativity* (Cambridge: Cambridge University Press, 1996).

Korsgaard, C. M., *Creating the Kingdom of Ends* (Cambridge: Cambridge University Press, 1996).

Krasnoff, L., 'Consensus, Stability and Normativity in Rawls's Political Liberalism', *The Journal of Philosophy*, **XCV**(6) (1998), 269–92.

Kymlicka, W., *Liberalism, Community and Culture* (Oxford: Clarendon Press, 1989).

Kymlicka, W., 'Liberal Individualism and Liberal Neutrality', *Ethics*, **99**(4) (1989), 83–105.

Kymlicka, W., *Contemporary Political Philosophy* (Oxford: Clarendon Press, 1990).

Lillehammer, H., 'The Doctrine of Internal Reasons', *The Journal of Value Inquiry*, **34**(4) (2000), 507–16.

Little, A., 'The Politics of Compensation: Tom Paine's *Agrarian Justice* and Liberal Egalitarianism', in A. Dobson and J. Stanyer (eds), *Contemporary Political Studies*, 1998, Vol. 2 (Proceedings of the Political Studies Association Annual Conference, 1998).

Lucas, J. R., 'The Philosophy of the Reasonable Man', *Philosophical Quarterly*, **13**(51) (1963), 97–106.

Lyons, D., 'Nature and Soundness of the Contract and Coherence Arguments', see in N. Daniels (ed.), *Reading Rawls*.

MacKinnon, C., *Only Words* (Cambridge, Mass.: Harvard University Press, 1993).

Malachowski, A. (ed.), *Reading Rorty* (Oxford: Blackwell, 1990).

Margalit, A., *The Decent Society* (Cambridge, Mass.: Harvard University Press, 1996).

Martin, M. W., *Self-Deception and Morality* (Kansas: University Press of Kansas, 1986).

Mason, A. (ed.), *Ideals of Equality* (Oxford: Blackwell, 1998).

Massey, S. J., 'Is Self-Respect a Moral or a Psychological Concept?', *Ethics*, **93** (1983), 246–61.

Massey, S. J., 'Kant on Self-Respect', *Journal of the History of Philosophy*, **21** (1983).

Matravers, M., *Justice and Punishment: The Rationale of Coercion* (Oxford: Oxford University Press, 2000).

Matravers, M., 'Responsibility, Luck, and the "Equality of What?" Debate', *Political Studies* (2002), forthcoming.

McCarthy, T., 'Kantian Constructivism and Reconstructivism: Rawls and Habermas in Dialogue', *Ethics*, **105** (1994), 44–63.

McKinnon, C., 'Self-Respect and the Stepford Wives', *Proceedings of the Aristotelian Society*, **XCVII** (1997), 325–30.

McKinnon, C., 'Review of *Towards Justice and Virtue* by Onora O'Neill', *Kantian Review*, **1** (1997), 171–6.

McKinnon, C., 'Rescue, Community, and Perfect Obligation', *Res Publica*, **6**(1) (2000), 105–16.

McKinnon, C., and Hampsher-Monk, I. (eds), *The Demands of Citizenship* (London and New York: Continuum, 2000).

McKinnon, C., 'Exclusion Rules and Self-Respect', *Journal of Value Inquiry*, **34** (2000), 491–505.

McKinnon, C., 'Justice for Vulnerable Agents: A Review of *The Bounds of Justice* by Onora O'Neill', *Imprints: A Journal of Analytical Socialism*, **5**(3) (2001), 251–60.

McKinnon, C., 'Rights: Their Basis and Limits', see in R. Bellamy and A. Mason (eds), *Political Concepts* (Manchester: Manchester University Press, 2002).

McKinnon, C., and Castiglione, D. (eds), *The Culture of Toleration in Diverse Societies: Reasonable Tolerance* (Manchester: Manchester University Press, 2002).

McPherson, M. S., 'Alternative Conceptions of Feasibility', see in D. Copp, J. Hampton and J. E. Roemer (eds), *The Idea of Democracy*.

Mendus, S., *Impartiality in Moral and Political Philosophy* (Oxford: Oxford University Press, 2002).

Meyers, D., 'The Politics of Self-Respect: A Feminist Perspective', *Hypatia*, 1(1) (1986), 83–100.

Meyers, D., *Self, Society and Personal Choice* (New York: Columbia University Press, 1988).

Meyers, D., 'Self-Respect and Autonomy', see in R. S. Dillon (ed.), *Dignity, Character and Self-Respect*.

Mill, J. S., *The Subjection of Women* (Indianapolis: Hackett Publishing Co., 1988).

Miller, D., 'Citizenship and Pluralism', *Political Studies*, 43(3) (1995), 432–50.

Miller, D., *On Nationality* (Oxford: Oxford University Press, 1997).

Miller, D., 'Equality and Justice', see in A. Mason (ed.), *Ideals of Equality*.

Modood, 'Muslims, Incitement to Hatred, and the Law', see in J. Horton (ed.), *Liberalism, Multiculturalism and Toleration*.

Moody-Adams, M., 'Race, Class, and the Social Construction of Self-Respect', see in R. S. Dillon (ed.), *Dignity, Character and Self-Respect*.

Moore, G. E., *Principia Ethica* (Cambridge: Cambridge University Press, 1986).

Mulhall, S., and Swift, A. (eds), *Liberals and Communitarians* (Oxford: Blackwell, 1992).

Nagel, T., 'Moral Conflict and Political Legitimacy', *Philosophy and Public Affairs*, 16(3) (1987), 215–40.

Nagel, T., 'Concealment and Exposure', *Philosophy and Public Affairs*, 27(1) (1998), 3–30.

Neblett, W., 'The Ethics of Guilt', *Journal of Philosophy*, 24 (1974), 652–63.

Norman, R., 'The Social Basis of Equality', see in A. Mason (ed.), *Ideals of Equality*.

Nozick, R., *Anarchy, State and Utopia* (Oxford: Blackwell, 1974).

O'Neill, O., *Constructions of Reason: Explorations of Kant's Practical Philosophy* (Cambridge: Cambridge University Press, 1989).

O'Neill, O., *Towards Justice and Virtue: A Constructive Account of Practical Reasoning* (Cambridge: Cambridge University Press, 1996).

O'Neill, O., 'Review of *Political Liberalism*', *The Philosophical Review*, 106(3) (1997), 411–28.

O'Neill, O., *Bounds of Justice* (Cambridge: Cambridge University Press, 2000).

O'Neill, O., 'Constructivism in Rawls and Kant', unpublished ms, on file with author.

Parker, H., *Instead of the Dole* (London: Routledge, 1989).

Paton, M., 'A Reconsideration of Kant's Treatment of Duties to Oneself', *Philosophical Quarterly*, 40 (1990), 222–33.

Paul, E. F., Miller, F., and Paul, J. (eds), *Altruism* (Cambridge: Cambridge University Press, 1993).

Pennock, J. R., and Chapman, J. W. (eds), *Nomos XXI: Compromise in Ethics, Law and Politics* (New York: New York University Press, 1979).

Pennock, J. R., and Chapman, J. W., *Justification: Nomos XXVIII* (New York: New York University Press, 1986).

Postow, B. C., 'Economic Dependence and Self-Respect', *The Philosophical Forum*, **X** (1978), 181–205.

Pritchard, M. S., 'Self-Regard and the Supererogatory', *Tulane Studies in Philosophy*, **31** (1982), 139–51.

Rawls, J., *A Theory of Justice* (Oxford: Oxford University Press, 1971).

Rawls, J., 'Fairness to Goodness', *Philosophical Review*, **84** (1975), 536–54.

Rawls, J., 'Kantian Constructivism in Moral Theory' (The Dewey Lectures), *Journal of Philosophy*, **77**(9) (1980), 515–72.

Rawls, J., 'Social Unity and Primary Goods', see in A. Sen and B. Williams (eds), *Utilitarianism and Beyond*.

Rawls, J., 'Justice as Fairness: Political not Metaphysical', *Philosophy and Public Affairs*, **14** (1985), 219–76.

Rawls, J., 'The Priority of the Right and Ideas of the Good', *Philosophy and Public Affairs*, **17**(4) (1988), 251–76.

Rawls, J., *Political Liberalism* (New York: Columbia University Press, 1993).

Rawls, J., 'Themes in Kant's Moral Philosophy', see in R. Beiner and W. J. Booth (eds), *Kant and Political Philosophy*.

Rawls, J., 'Reply to Habermas', *The Journal of Philosophy*, **XCII**(3) (1995), 132–80.

Rawls, J., 'The Idea of Public Reason Revisited', *The University of Chicago Law Review*, **64**(3) (1997), 765–807.

Rawls, J., *Collected Papers* (ed. S. Freeman) (Cambridge, Mass.: Harvard University Press, 1999).

Rawls, J., *The Law of Peoples* (Cambridge, Mass.: Harvard University Press, 1999).

Rawls, J., *Justice as Fairness: A Restatement* (Cambridge, Mass.: Harvard University Press, 2001).

Raz, J., *The Morality of Freedom* (Oxford: Clarendon Press, 1986).

Raz, J., 'Facing Diversity: The Case of Epistemic Abstinence', *Philosophy and Public Affairs*, **19**(1) (1990), 3–46.

Raz, J., *Ethics in the Public Domain* (Oxford: Clarendon Press, 1994).

Raz, J., 'The Amoralist', see in G. Cullity and B. Gaus (eds), *Ethics and Practical Reason*.

Reath, A., Herman, B., and Korsgaard, C. M. (eds), *Reclaiming the History of Ethics: Essays for John Rawls* (Cambridge: Cambridge University Press, 1997).

Rhode, D., 'Association and Assimilation', *Northwestern University Law Review*, **106** (1986), 106–45.

Richards, V. (ed.), *Why Work?* (London: Freedom Press, 1983).

Richardson, H. S., 'Beyond Good and Right: Toward a Constructive Pragmatism', *Philosophy and Public Affairs*, **24**(2) (1995), 108–41.

Roemer, J. E., 'The Morality and Efficiency of Market Socialism', *Ethics*, **102**(3) (1992), 448–64.

Roemer, J. E., 'The Possibility of Market Socialism', see in D. Copp, J. Hampton and J. E. Roemer (eds), *The Idea of Democracy*.

Rorty, R., *Contingency, Irony, Solidarity* (Cambridge: Cambridge University Press, 1989).

Rorty, R., *Objectivity, Relativism and Truth* (Cambridge: Cambridge University Press, 1991).

Rorty, R., *Philosophy and Social Hope* (London: Penguin Books, 1999).

Rosenblum, N., *Membership and Morals: The Personal Uses of Pluralism in America* (Princeton, NJ: Princeton University Press, 1998).

Russell, B., 'In Praise of Idleness', see in V. Richards (ed.), *Why Work?*.

Sachs, D., 'How to Distinguish Self-Respect from Self-Esteem', *Philosophy and Public Affairs*, **10**(4) (1981), 346–60.

Sachs, D., 'Self-Respect and Respect for Others: Are They Independent?', *Tulane Studies in Philosophy*, **31** (1982), 109–28.

Sandel, M. J., *Liberalism and the Limits of Justice* (Cambridge: Cambridge University Press, 1982).

Sayre-McCord, G. (ed.), *Essays on Moral Realism* (Ithaca: Cornell University Press, 1988).

Scanlon, T., 'Contractualism and Utilitarianism', see in A. Sen and B. Williams (eds), *Utilitarianism and Beyond*.

Scanlon, T. M., *What We Owe to Each Other* (Cambridge, Mass.: Harvard University Press, 1998).

Scarre, G., 'Utilitarianism and Self-Respect', *Utilitas*, **4** (1) (1992), 27–42.

Scheffler, S., 'The Appeal of Political Liberalism', *Ethics*, **105** (1994), 4–22.

Sencerz, S., 'Moral Intuitions and Justification in Ethics', *Philosophical Studies*, **50** (1986), 77–95.

Sen, A. and Williams, B. (eds), *Utilitarianism and Beyond* (Cambridge: Cambridge University Press, 1982).

Sher, G., *Beyond Neutrality: Perfectionism and Politics* (Cambridge: Cambridge University Press, 1997).

Shklar, J., *Ordinary Vices* (Cambridge, Mass.: Belknap Press, 1984).

Shoemaker, D. W., 'Theoretical Persons and Practical Agents', *Philosophy and Public Affairs*, **25**(4) (1996), 318–32.

Shue, H., 'Liberty and Self-Respect', *Ethics*, **85** (1975), 195–203.

Sibley, W. M., 'The Rational Versus the Reasonable', *Philosophical Review*, **62** (1953), 554–60.

Simmons, A. John, 'Justification and Legitimacy', *Ethics*, **109** (1999), 739–71.

Sinopoli, R. C., 'Thick-Skinned Liberalism: Redefining Civility', *American Political Science Review*, **89**(3) (1995), 612–20.

Smart, J. J. C., 'Reason and Conduct', *Philosophy*, **25** (1950), 209–24.

Steiner, H., *An Essay on Rights* (London: Blackwell, 1994).

Taylor, C., *Human Agency and Language: Philosophical Papers Vol. 1* (Cambridge: Cambridge University Press, 1985).

Taylor, C., *Philosophy and the Human Sciences: Philosophical Papers Vol. 2* (Cambridge: Cambridge University Press, 1985).

Taylor, G., *Pride, Shame and Guilt* (Oxford: Clarendon Press, 1985).

Taylor, G., 'Shame, Integrity and Self-Respect', see in R. S. Dillon (ed.), *Dignity, Character and Self-Respect*.

Telfer, E., 'Self-Respect', *Philosophical Quarterly*, **18** (1968), 114–21.

Thomas, L. L., 'Self-Respect: Theory and Practice', see in R. S. Dillon (ed.), *Dignity, Character and Self-Respect*.

Thomas, L. L., 'Morality and Our Self-Concept', *Journal of Value Inquiry*, **12** (1978), 258–68.

Tomasi, J., 'Kymlicka, Liberalism and Respect for Cultural Minorities', *Ethics*, **105** (1995), 580–603.

Torisky Jnr., E. V., 'Van Parijs, Rawls and Unconditional Basic Income', *Analysis*, **53**(4) (1993), 289–97.

Van der Veen, R., 'Real Freedom vs. Reciprocity: Competing Views on the Justice of Unconditional Basic Income', *Political Studies*, **XLVI**(1) (1998), 140–63.

Van Parijs, P., 'Why Surfers Should Be Fed: The Liberal Case for an Unconditional Basic Income', *Philosophy and Public Affairs*, **20**(4) (1991), 101–31.

Van Parijs, P., 'Basic Income Capitalism', *Ethics*, **102**(3) (1992), 465–84.

Van Parijs, P. (ed.), *Arguing for Basic Income* (London: Verso, 1992).

Van Parijs, P., *Real Freedom for All. What (if anything) Can Justify Capitalism?* (Oxford: Clarendon Press, 1995).

Van Parijs, P., 'Reciprocity and the Justification of an Unconditional Basic Income. Reply to Stuart White', *Political Studies*, **45**(2) (1997), 327–30.

Velleman, D., 'What Happens When Someone Acts?', *Mind*, **101**(403) (1992), 461–81.

Velleman, D., 'The Possibility of Practical Reason', *Ethics*, **106** (1996), 694–726.

Waldron, J., 'Theoretical Foundations of Liberalism', *Philosophical Quarterly*, **37** (1987), 127–50.

Waldron, J., 'Legislation and Moral Neutrality', see in R. E. Goodin and A. Reeve (eds), *Liberal Neutrality*.

Waldron, J., *Liberal Rights: Collected Papers 1981–1991* (Cambridge: Cambridge University Press, 1993).

Walzer, M., *Spheres of Justice* (Oxford: Martin Robertson, 1983).

Wenar, L., '*Political Liberalism*: An Internal Critique', *Ethics*, **106** (1995), 32–62.

White, S., 'Freedom of Association and the Right to Exclude', *Journal of Political Philosophy*, 5(4) (1997), 373–91.

White, S., 'Liberal Equality, Exploitation, and the Case for an Unconditional Basic Income', *Political Studies*, **45**(2) (1997), 312–26.

White, S., 'What Do Egalitarians Want?', see in J. Franklin (ed.), *Equality*.

Williams, B., *Morality: An Introduction* (Cambridge: Cambridge University Press, 1972).

Williams, B., *Problems of the Self* (Cambridge: Cambridge University Press, 1973).

Williams, B., *Moral Luck: Philosophical Papers 1973–1980* (Cambridge: Cambridge University Press, 1981).

Williams, B., *Ethics and the Limits of Philosophy* (London: Fontana Press, 1982).
Williams, B., *Shame and Necessity* (Berkeley: University of California Press, 1993).
Williams, B., *Making Sense of Humanity* (Cambridge: Cambridge University Press, 1995).
Williams, B., 'Forward to Basics', see in J. Franklin (ed.), *Equality*.
Williams, H., 'Kant, Rawls, Habermas and the Metaphysics of Justice', *Kantian Review*, **3** (1999), 1–17.
Wolff, J., *Robert Nozick: Property, Justice and the Minimal State* (Cambridge: Polity Press, 1991).
Wolff, J., 'Fairness, Respect and the Egalitarian Ethos', *Philosophy and Public Affairs*, **27** (1998), 99–122.
Yanal, R. J., 'Self-Esteem', *Noûs*, **21** (1987), 363–79.
Young, I. M., 'Polity and Group Difference: A Critique of the Ideal of Universal Citizenship', *Ethics*, **99** (1989), 250–74.

Index